ALBIE SACHS

The Soft Vengeance
of a
Freedom Fighter

NEW EDITION

Foreword by
DESMOND TUTU

Introduction by
NANCY SCHEPER-HUGHES

D0017364

UNIVERSITY OF CALIFORNIA PRESS

Berkeley Los Angeles London

University of California Press
Berkeley and Los Angeles, California

University of California Press, Ltd.
London, England
First California Paperback 2000

First published in Great Britain by
Grafton Books 1990

First paperback published in Great Britain by
Paladin 1991

Library of Congress Cataloging-in-Publication Data

Sachs, Albie, 1935–
    The soft vengeance of a freedom fighter / Albie Sachs ; foreword
by Desmond Tutu, introduction by Nancy Scheper-Hughes.
        p.   cm.
    Originally published : Cape Town : David Philip, 1990. With new
foreword and introduction.
    ISBN 0–520–22019–6 (alk. paper)
    1. Sachs, Albie, 1935—Health. 2. Amputees—Mozambique
Biography. 3. Physically handicapped—Mozambique Biography.
4. Lawyers—Mozambique Biography.   I. Title.
RD796.S23A3   2000
362.4'092—dc21
[B]   99–34214
                                                          CIP

The Soft Vengeance of a Freedom Fighter

CONTENTS

Foreword to the New Edition

Sometimes when I have felt a little depressed I would go to Parliament to sit in the public gallery and look down at all those "terrorists" now occupying the government benches. It is something to lift the heaviest heart to behold those who were regarded by the previous apartheid government as the most dangerous terrorists, and who now, in the new democratic dispensation, are the Hon. Minister of this or that. I would recall that some of them were fellow marchers in rallies against the awfulness of apartheid, and with some we were targets for teargassing, and now here they are, members of a democratically elected National Assembly.

Sitting in the government ranks, now a member of the African National Congress, was Melanie Verwoerd. Can you believe it—the granddaughter-in-law of the high priest and architect of apartheid, Dr. H. F. Verwoerd himself. Possibly he was turning in his grave at this extraordinary paradox in a land of many strange ironies and paradoxes.

Sitting in the front row there you could see Dullah Omar, now Minister of Justice. Just a few years earlier he was harassed by the apartheid state and refused a passport at the very last moment before his departure to take up a prestigious scholarship in law at the University of London.

To illustrate some of the paradoxes of our beloved South Africa, he had been on the death list of the CCB, the quaintly named Security Service assassination unit. He had a heart condition and they decided to do him in by swapping his heart tablets. Sometimes the agents of darkness are unusually inept, and on this occasion they failed in their designs. Minister Omar was to pilot through Parliament legislation that brought the Truth and Reconciliation Commission into being, and one of its purposes was to grant amnesty to those who had committed politically motivated crimes. Dullah Omar produced the law that would grant amnesty for those who had tried to kill him.

Albie Sachs was nearly assassinated by a powerful car bomb in Mozambique. He lost most of his right arm and the sight of one eye. He should by rights have been consumed by a burning desire to get even with those who had planned this dastardly deed. Instead he came to play a central role in the negotiations that helped to produce South Africa's new and much admired constitution, which is pivotal to the new democracy that has come into being with the transition from the repression of apartheid to the freedom of justice.

In the South Africa of old, Parliament had been sovereign. It could—and did—pass all sorts of extraordinary laws in which, more often than not, the gulf between legality on one side and morality or goodness or justice on the other seemed unbridgeable. In the new order the constitution is supreme, and it is a constitution held in high regard in most parts of the world for its adherence to the tenets of the universal declaration of human rights. This means that even the perpetrators of the old order and its staunchest supporters were decreed to have inalienable rights, most of which they had assiduously denied their opponents when they were in power: the rights to freedom of expression, a fair trial, freedom from torture, etc. Albie Sachs was passionate in ensuring that the new South Africa would cultivate a culture of respect for human rights, which must of necessity be universal and so would apply to those who had tried to kill him.

And he has been appointed a judge of the Constitutional Court, the highest court in the land. One of its first acts was to declare unconstitutional a presidential decree that affected the powers of the provinces. It actually found against President

Nelson Mandela and in favor of those who advocate a form of federalism, even though most of these are former supporters of the apartheid dispensation—and Albie Sachs is a member of that court which made such a ruling. Now, that is something! Humanly speaking, you would want to let them get their comeuppance. But no, that is what we struggled for, that is what he lost his arm for, that is what it was all about—to bring into being this new kind of society, this new kind of South Africa where the rule of law obtains, in contrast to the former times when the rule of law was horribly abrogated: a new kind of society that speaks of the sanctity of the rights of human beings, of all human beings, even those who had done the utmost to deny such rights to those they had arbitrarily excluded. That, for Albie Sachs, was his vengeance, his soft vengeance. Perhaps it is revenge to let someone who hates beautiful things sit in a gorgeous garden—but it is not a destructive vengeance, for he may one day be converted, and so you may destroy the enemy by making him into a friend.

I found this a deeply moving account—so utterly frank, revealing his vulnerable self, warts and all. It is so beautiful, almost poetic, in describing the sense of his body, his sheer physicality, the role women have played in helping him come in touch with his body, helping him to become whole. And a wonderful ending, a beautiful tribute to his mother.

Those who might still be inclined to criticize the Truth and Reconciliation Commission would do well to read Albie's justification for this way of dealing with the past.

Another paradox—Albie Sachs's meditation on the significance of the voting cross—coming from a Jew it is deeply moving to think of that mark on the ballot paper and the cross of sacrifice. This book ought to be a best seller.

Desmond Tutu
Archbishop Emeritus

Introduction to the New Edition

Sacred Wounds: Writing with the Body

NANCY SCHEPER-HUGHES

You cannot avoid them for they are present at every political event. Father Michael Lapsley with his startling metal hooks where his hands should be. . . . There he is right now mischievously lighting a young woman's cigarette (a magician's trick!) or, over there, skillfully holding the stem of a wine glass raised in a defiant toast. Once the shock leaves one wants to caress his gentle hook-hand, and to return the toast, with wine goblets raised high, clinking glass with metal and champagne with tears. And over there, his back turned so carelessly to the door, is Albie Sachs with his handsomely lined face and his resonant soothing voice, the agnostics' theologian, dressed in his priestly robes, his favorite bright daṣhiki, excitedly waving his phantom limb, to make a point. That ever-present missing piece is Albie's most expressive body part, that freely waving sleeve is Albie's sweet banner of liberty. Of thee, I sing. Albie. (Field notes, Cape Town, 15 February 1994)

In the presence of Justice Albie Sachs one wants to be a traditional praise singer in the Xhosa warrior tradition of South Africa. Draped in leopard skins and waving a ritual baton, one wants to leap and dart while loudly chanting Albie's many virtues—his courage and strength under fire, his fierce intelligence, his unassailable dignity, and his gentle, sometimes self-mocking, humor. Or, in the classical tradition of Virgil's *Aeneid* (*"Arma virumque cano . . . ."*) one wants to sing of "arms and a man who came to [these] shores." And thereby honor the man, Albert Louis Sachs, born of workaday but politically inspired immigrant Lithuanian Jewish parents, who is today one of his new country's national treasures, a man for whom the proverbial bells rang, the drums beat, and the militant "young lions" of the townships roared when after a quarter of a century of exile he returned home to the beloved country a wounded, but victorious, ANC warrior.

Albie Sachs's personal odyssey—from privileged white South African schoolboy in camp shorts in the early 1940s, to skeptical and mildly rebellious university student in the late 1950s, to civil rights lawyer and civil rights activist in the late 1950s, to political dissident and political prisoner, twice detained in the mid 1960s, to long-exiled ANC activist in London and Mozambique and one of the apartheid Security Force's most wanted "race traitors," to mature writer of lyrical autobiographical books banned by soulless South African civil servants, who were as terrified of beauty, openness, and tenderness as they were of armed insurrection, to judge in the highest court in the new South Africa—is the story in microcosm of the antiapartheid struggle and its glorious resolution.

But how to describe Albie Sachs to an American audience with political sentiments and cultural sensibilities so very much at odds with this reserved, mild-mannered, yet morally—and politically—severe English-speaking white man with an African soul? Albie is both the archetypal twentieth-century revolutionary and the classical Enlightenment modernist: a defender of the right to bear arms against a tyrannical and racist state and a firm believer in reason and rationality, in structure and form, in social planning, and in the positive power of "the state" and traditional institutions—law, medicine, architecture, the academy—to uplift and liberate all people. Albie is perhaps more Thomas Paine or Roger Casement than Abraham Lincoln or Martin Luther King. A gentle freedom fighter and a tough negotiator, he is a man of many and often contradictory stripes. He is a warm, direct, and generously intimate diarist, willing to share with anonymous readers some of the most intimate, even embarrassing or slightly compromising moments of his wounding and recovery. His body and its tactics are rendered almost shockingly public, but what might have been a personal confession, a private memoir of suffering and victimhood, is artfully transformed into a bold and daring revolutionary act. Albie's body is deployed as both sign and a symbol of the struggle years and the subsequent search for collective remorse and reconciliation.

On first meeting the narrator of *Soft Vengeance,* one is immediately brought up short. For in person Albie Sachs is a formidable, guarded, and intensely private person. He can be quite a severe taskmaster, quick to correct and even rebuke the thoughtless or irresponsible comment. He can seem all business and not much given to small talk or pleasantries. But then, as Scrooge's ghost would say, *mankind* is his business, and one is more forgiving of his sometimes "difficult" self. Albie's smile is public but his feelings, dreams, and wishes of the soul are securely locked away. Awaiting his next diary perhaps. For one who has seduced so many readers with the moving and intimate details of his painfully difficult recovery, his re-learning to walk, sit, bathe, and write with one arm, Albie avoids drawing attention to himself in public. He agonizes about whether or not to remove his shirt on a beautiful, brilliantly hot summer day while sitting on a park bench in Cape Town, lest the sight of his wound detract from the pleasure of nearby picnickers on the grass. Another part of Albie deeply resents attention drawn to his missing part, wanting to keep his body to himself, even though he himself has made his body into a public issue.

Albie Sachs is a child of struggle to the core. Birthday celebrations are for the bourgeoisie, for those with nothing better to do with their lives than mark dead time passed. So, he summarily, perhaps even a little rudely, rejects a surprise birthday cake presented in his honor during a visit to Berkeley, and he adamantly refuses to blow out the candles, leaving it to the somewhat confused hosts and their other guests. But, while refusing a birthday celebration for himself, Albie could throw himself with pleasure into the spontaneous late night birthday party for the ANC's chief negotiator, Cyril Ramaphosa, marking the end of the long, tense meetings in Kempton Park, Johannesburg, that paved the way in 1994 for the adoption of the new Constitution for a democratic South Africa. The local media captured indelible images of that extraordinary party and of Albie Sachs—in a glorious state of abandonment—dancing with the enemy, the same dour officials of the old National Party who had just a few years earlier put a bounty on his head.

Courage in the Body

In this new paperback edition of *The Soft Vengeance of a Freedom Fighter,* Albie Sachs gives us an achingly beautiful and poetic account of his near death at the hands of the South African apartheid state, presented as a parable of the wounding and recovery of his beloved native country. Like most ignominious acts of political terrorism, the one recounted here took but a few seconds, though Albie will have to live with it for the rest of his days. On a clear April morning in 1988, as Albie was getting ready for his usual jog along the sandy beaches of Maputo in Mozambique, he opened the trunk of his car to remove a blanket and a thermos of tea, and an apartheid maniac's bomb exploded into his life.

For the next several months Sachs's political courage and optimism had to be put at the service of his own recovery, in meeting all the mundane demands of living and dealing with a damaged body/self. Sitting up, dragging himself to the edge of his hospital bed, using a commode, pulling himself up on his feet, staging a balancing act on a painfully damaged heel, forcing his left hand to do the bidding that had always come so naturally to his right hand, initially making one eye serve for two, all of these hospital bed struggles become focused acts of political resistance. "I will be back, I will complete my run on the beach!" is Albie's revolutionary battle cry as he is wheeled out of the clinic in Mozambique on his way to England for complicated surgeries. The fulfillment of that promise is just one of Albie's sweet moments of "soft vengeance" against those who would have blown him to kingdom come in order to protect their white privileges, their second and third summer and winter vacation homes, their private swimming pools, their black-chauffeured cars.

If Albie, the agnostic Jew, will forgive me, *Soft Vengeance* reads for me like nothing quite so much as a chapter from *The Lives of the Saints* I was brought up on as a child. And of these his tale most resembles the "little way" of Saint Teresa of Lisieux: her daily battles against irritation and annoyance at the stupidity and cupidity of her "fellow" nuns, her mundane crises with "the Lord of all these pots and pans and things" as she gradually learns to accept her limited ministry even in the convent kitchen. And all the while, in this claustrophobic social world, as confining for St. Teresa as Albie's hospital bed was for him, she develops a clarity of vision and a sure-footed path to sisterly/brotherly love and generosity of spirit that would serve equally well in the cloisters as in the worldly battle against social injustice. Similarly, Albie's "little way" and his clarity of vision comes from making his personal recovery in the hospital and on the beach into an embrace of the new political future of South Africa. His recovery becomes a paragon of political and moral virtue for a time of healing and renewal.

Albie—no ordinary "hero" or "saint" (and he would most vigorously reject both these labels)—recently shared with Harry Kreisler in a videotaped conversation at the University of California, Berkeley, that the books that most inspired him as a child, and that years later often sustained him as a political activist, were fairy tales and legends, stories of young men challenged with impossible trials, climbing a glass mountain to reach the princess, clearing the underbrush of enchanted forests, "stories of love and endurance." These inchoate early images, said Albie, helped during his own periods of struggle: "I remember that sensation of pushing and pushing, and withstanding the pressures on you to succumb. And of winning!" Elsewhere, he described the crux of it all: "I suppose that the fundamental puzzle that one lives with is the whole question of the role of will, the place in life of volition and choice."

One recalls from Albie Sachs's first memoir, *The Jail Diary of Albie Sachs,* how much he had relied on the smallest bodily pleasures during his 167 days of solitary confinement—picking sand out of a comb, hanging up his pants in fanciful patterns, hunting and killing fleas—to keep himself sane. And one remembers Albie's vanity in having once admired the elegant shape of his "barrister's hands" when, suddenly and out of the blue Mozambican sky, one of those lovely hands is ripped away forever. Those simple pleasures and that same courage in the body return again here. And so, to his delight, Albie notes that as his right-handedness necessarily shifts to left, a softer and more feminine side of himself is liberated. His wounded body is more immediately receptive to human touch, and he delights in his own purely embodied existence.

In the topsy-turvy world of the hospital bed, the cognitive gives way to the sensual and the sentient. There is a Cartesian "revolution" from top-to-bottom self-consciousness: "I shit therefore I am!" and "good old cock!" says Albie with a mischievous grin. And so, with humor and a paradoxical ambidexterity, Albie rearms himself in his hospital room in preparation for his own and his country's almost certain victory against the forces of race oppression—the real "soft vengeance" of this political morality tale.

Social Suffering

In recent years an anthropology of suffering has emerged as a new kind of theodicy, a cultural inquiry into the ways that people attempt to explain the presence of pain, affliction, and evil in the world. At times of crisis, in moments of intense suffering, people everywhere demand an answer to the primal existential question: "Why me, oh God? Why me, of all people? Why now?" The quest for meaning may be posed to vindicate an indifferent God, to quell one's self doubt, or to restore faith in an orderly and righteous world. As Clifford Geertz once noted, the one thing humans seem unable to accept is the idea of the world as deficient in meaning.

Albie Sachs and his comrades never had to raise the "Why me? Why now?" question. They knew they would be imprisoned, tortured, and mutilated by the police state; those were the implicit rules, after all, of the revolutionary struggle. The stakes were incredibly high. And, consequently, this is anything other than a victim story. It is the story of a happy victor. In the context of the struggle for the soul of South Africa, the attempt on his life and his wounding is treated by Albie Sachs almost like a stroke of good fortune. He could have been dead, after all, and unable to witness the glorious transition that was— as he reminds us in the epilogue—no miracle at all but the result of one of the most planned and strategized revolutions in modern history.

The quest to "make sense" of suffering, wounding, and premature death is as old as Job, and as fraught with moral ambiguity. Just as the companions of Job return to taunt him, to demand an explanation for his suffering ("You must have sinned"), friends and relatives of prisoners of conscience kidnapped and tortured often hint: "You must have been into something. You must have deserved it." And just as Job steadfastly refuses the temptation to self-blame, insisting that he was a just man, Albie Sachs eloquently protests that he and his ANC comrades suffered (and some died) "because we were good, because we were on the side of the angels."

The ability to turn bad into good is a sign of resilience and necessary for healing, and is aided immeasurably by strong religious faith or political convictions. Father Michael Lapsley, who was the recipient in 1990 of a deadly letter bomb from some still unidentified would-be assassins, insists he is a victor and not a victim of the apartheid state that tried to kill him. In living he defeats evil and death. And Father Lapsley believes that he was never closer to God than in the almost transcendent moment of the blast that took away an eye and both his hands: "I sensed the presence of the Holy Spirit accompanying me at that moment," he told me in 1994. During a visit to Canaan Baptist Church of Christ on 116th Street in Harlem, Lapsley told the congregation: "I stand before you as a sign of what apartheid has done . . . but also as a sign of the power of God to heal, the power of love, of gentleness, of compassion. The power of light is stronger than the power of darkness, and in the power of God we shall be victorious."

The wounded body often becomes a template of individual and collective memory, both a map and a moral charter. Michael Lapsley gestures broadly with his metal hooks, referring to them as his "entree" into the black community. "These," he told me recently, gesturing to his hooks, "are the gold standard. They open up many doors into South African township life." Similarly, Albie's injury is a sacred wound, a red badge of courage, a visible symbol of the pact he struck as a negative intellectual (in Gramsci's sense) and as a "race/class traitor" to white South Africa. While it (quite literally) "unbalanced" him, the loss of his arm in that car blast provided one of the grounds for his "certainty" in the body and in the newly emerging body politic.

Albie's understanding of his loss and its meaning is of a more phenomenological order. His particular sensibility and his approach to writing and thinking through the medium of the body is reminiscent of another ethnographer of the mindful body, Oliver Sacks. Both Sacks and Sachs share an intuitively

Wittgensteinian perception that all knowledge and all certainty begin with the "unquestionability" of the body. "If you know that here is one hand," Wittegenstein began his last book, *On Certainty,* "we'll grant you all the rest." This generative perception of the "givenness" of the body as a natural tool or a natural symbol with which to "think" the world came to Wittgenstein while he was working as a volunteer with patients hospitalized during World War I. Wittgenstein's essay is in part a reflection on the circumstances or the situations which might take away one's certainty of the body and all that this implies. ("If here you know there is *no* hand . . . or leg . . . or eye. . . .")

A worthy heir of Wittgenstein's philosophical reflections, *Soft Vengeance,* more than any of the recent books that deal with the body in pain, returns us to the everyday, existential grounds of the body as lived and experienced in a particular self at a particular historical moment. If the body is text, it is certainly a great deal more than that. In this magnificently concrete and generously and vulnerably frank and intimate narrative of his body in pain, Albie Sachs tells the story of the antiapartheid struggle, the courage of the comrades, their certainty in the moral goodness and rightness of their cause, their willingness to suffer the consequences of their political commitment, and the political and existential meanings of "putting one's body on the line."

In Sachs's moral world and in his generous political vision, almost anything that can bind former enemies into the semblance of a "normal," civil, and democratic society—even if it means granting amnesty to one's torturers or sharing an impoverished metaphor like "post-traumatic stress disorder" with one's police captors—will do.

Undoing

The romance with remorse and with reparation, memory, and healing—in both the individual and the social body—has emerged as a master narrative of the late twentieth century, as both individuals and entire nations struggle to overcome the legacies of suffering ranging from rape and domestic violence to collective atrocities of state-sponsored dirty wars and ethnic cleansings. The psychologies of remorse, guilt, catharsis, and closure compete today with the theologies of reconciliation, forgiveness, and redemption in another version of what Philippe Reiff called the triumph of the therapeutic.

Michael Ignatieff has hit upon an appropriate generative metaphor for looking at the present contexts of national recovery: *getting over*. The words conjure up Biblical images of safe passage, of reaching the other side, and, finally, of *overcoming*. Just what needs to be "gotten over" if South Africa and South Africans are to get safely to the other side? Is reconciliation possible without some kind of powerful, transcendental faith? For many South Africans the first step in the cultural politics of reconciliation and forgiveness is knowledge-seeking, learning exactly what happened to whom, by whom, and why.

"I sometimes wonder," Michael Lapsley said 1997, "just who that man or woman was who typed my name on the envelope that was supposed to kill me. And I wonder what they told their spouses or children that night at supper time about what they did in the office that day. Either they are so dehumanized that they don't care or else they have learned to live comfortably with their guilt. . . . I don't want vengeance but I think that the names and faces of these people should be known." In his epilogue, Albie Sachs is equally bedeviled by both wanting and not wanting to know the names and the details of his would-be assassins.

Those seeking truth in South Africa today do not want the partial, indeterminate, shifting "truths" of the postmodernist, but the sweet, "objective" truth of the moralist, and with it a restored sense of wholeness and a taste of justice. The official vehicle for that collective soul-searching, "getting over," and liberating the country of the ghosts of its past is the Truth and Reconciliation Commission. One of the first times I met Albie Sachs was during a special, closed conference on "Justice in Transition," held at the Lord Charles Hotel in Somerset West, Cape Town. It was the first of two meetings held to consider just what kind of truth commission and what sort of amnesty would be granted to both the apartheid and antiapartheid "operatives"—without in any way equating the struggles of each side—in the process of nation-building and social healing. Human rights abuses had been committed on both sides and hitherto silent victims had to be given a chance to speak. At a panel featuring four South Africans who had suffered at the hands of the apartheid state, Albie spoke brilliantly about remorse and forgiveness. He was followed by an apartheid widow, Nomonde Calata, whose husband was one of the "Cradock Four" murdered after a political meeting in Port Elizabeth. Unaccustomed to public speaking, Nomonde broke down in telling how her eight-year-old child kept asking where her daddy had gone. Albie rose from his chair and stepped over to protect and enfold the grieving woman in a warm embrace that was at once spontaneous and true, a wordless gesture that reminded the diverse and somewhat contentious international group of former dissidents and freedom fighters of the importance of a public recognition of personal grief.

On 30 October 1998, the TRC officially concluded its four-year investigation based on hundreds of hearings around the country at which thousands of victims of apartheid-era brutality, and a much smaller number of perpetrators of apartheid terror and violence, told their stories. The devil that tortured South Africans, including Albie Sachs, is found in the details of the final 3,500-page report. Although details of that report are already being contested, the fact that political parties and individuals across the political spectrum—from P. W. Botha and F. W. de Klerk to the new South African President, Thabo

Mbeki—are protesting aspects of its findings will be seen by most people as a stamp of credibility on the entire process. And, as Albie Sachs noted during his Regents Professorship lecture on "Violence and Recovery," in the end the value of the TRC proceedings will be in asking all South Africans to settle for an agreed upon, a "good enough" truth—a central narrative that will at the very least place black and white South Africans, Afrikaners and English-speakers, Xhosas and Zulus, ANC and PAC members on the same map rather than living in different nations across the road from each other.

Surprised by Joy

Among Albie Sachs's many gifts as a person and as a narrator is his quiet and unassuming sense of joy and his studied wonder in the given, created world and its many small and unassuming pleasures, so many of which were interrupted by the attack on his life. In reading this book, and reflecting on the changes that have come to pass in the new South Africa, one can only conclude that Justice Albie Sachs is a very happy man. In his lifetime he has managed to write two paradoxically happy books about two hideous experiences. And just as Albie opened his prison book with his sense of delight in having a flush toilet provided by the anal-compulsive Afrikaner police in his tiny prison cell, he opens this second political-autobiographical book with a "politically incorrect" ethnic joke, an old one even I recall from my Brooklyn childhood days. The one about Himie Cohen falling off a bus, dusting himself, and making the sign of the cross. With this joke as background, Albie tells how he first explored his body in the hospital in Maputo following surgery to see how much of himself is still there, and how much is missing. And he is almost giddy, a little high on having so very nearly escaped death.

Albie's happiness comes from knowing that he was on the side of the angels in this struggle against the white South African state. A deeply reflexive and philosophical man who probably, under more "normal" circumstances, might have been given to bouts of existential doubt, angst, and depression, he thrives on his faith in the struggle and in the good company of his comrades who are perhaps even more than a family to him. The question he poses for himself—and answers in the new epilogue—is whether he can bear to live happily in more ordinary and "boring" times. Can he be weaned from "the struggle," can he make the transition from "freedom fighter" to ordinary citizen? One of his very few expressed moments of doubt comes immediately following the democratic elections in April 1994. What more was there to live for?

In his poignant epilogue, Albie shows—through a series of personal vignettes about the elections, his refusal of political office, his appointment as judge to the Constitutional Court of South Africa, his anxious swearing-in ceremony ("I raised my stump: 'So help me God.' "), his role in the formation of the Truth and Reconciliation Commission, his complicated granting and withholding of forgiveness to an ordinary Afrikaner "by-stander" seeking reconciliation with the past, his desire to know and refusal to know the volunteered and contradictory "facts" about the men who planned his death—how a tortured individual and a tortured new state manage to go about building a new and ordinary, hopefully even banal, life.

And Albie shows just what there is for "an old warrior" to live for in the new South Africa: the serenity that comes from having been one of the writers of the new Constitution, now in the enviable position of being able to interpret and defend it; the quiet joy of knowing that a Bill of Rights has replaced White Rights; the joy of witnessing electric lights going on and water taps opening up in squatter camps and townships that surround all of South Africa's major cities.

Albie's quiet happiness is, finally, that of the returned exile who is able to relocate in a hillside cottage in his beloved childhood home in Clifton by the sea. Of listening to jazz at open cafés on weekend nights along the wharf in Cape Town. In beginning a new relationship with a beautiful, smart, and gentle woman. Albie is a happy man because his country has opened up, and what was small was made large, what was crooked was made straight, what was rigid and dead has become fluid and lively. Albie is happy because he wanted to be a freedom fighter and he *was* a freedom fighter. And now that he is a judge in the highest court of the land he lets us know (through marvelous asides based on an attempt to gather his mother's life history before she died) that maybe his dear mother, wherever her soul rests, is very happy too.

Preface

I think if somehow I could miraculously be offered my arm back, I would refuse. I get a shock sometimes when I see a photograph of myself with no hand protruding from my right sleeve. Even the incompleteness of my bouncing shadow as I walk along a bumpy mountain trail can startle me. Yet I feel totally embodied in my new physical self, and know that even if my volition were to seek to reverse the narrative of my life, my shape has become irrecuperably embedded in the forward momentum of my country. I am so habituated to living in the world as I am that I doubt that I could stand the trauma of being restored to my previous self. Not that I don't have any problems when looking at pictures of myself "before the bomb." I love the seriousness of that younger guy—the thick, curly, long hair, the sense of strain and endeavor, the self-conscious eagerness of his evident comradeship, the hopeful radiance that at times infuriated his friends who were convinced it invited martyrdom rather than glory, and then felt that their direst forebodings had materialized when they read that he had been blown up by a car bomb. Was it worth it?—to this day they look without looking and ask without asking—was it worth it?

The Soft Vengeance of a Freedom Fighter

1

Oh shit. Everything has abruptly gone dark, I am feeling strange and cannot see anything. The beach, I am going to the beach, I packed a frosty beer for after my run, something is wrong. Oh shit, I must have banged my head, like I used to do when climbing Table Mountain in Cape Town, dreaming of the struggle, and cracking my cranium against an overhang. It will go away, I must just be calm and wait. Watered the tropical pot-plants, stared at the ten heads on the giant African sculpture in my beautiful apartment. Oh shit, how can I be so careless? The darkness is not clearing, this is something serious, a terrible thing is happening to me, I am swirling, I cannot steady myself as I wait for consciousness and light to return. I feel a shuddering punch against the back of my neck, and then what seems like another one. The sense of threat gets stronger and stronger, I am being dominated, overwhelmed. I have to fight, I have to resist. I can feel arms coming from behind me, pulling at me under my shoulders. I am being kidnapped, they have come from Pretoria to drag me over the border and interrogate me and lock me up. This is the moment we have all been waiting for, the few ANC members still working in Mozambique, with dread and yet with a weird kind of eagerness.

'Leave me,' I yell out. 'Leave me.'

I jerk my shoulders and thrash my arms as violently as I can. I always wondered how I would react, whether I would fight physically, risking death, or whether I would go quietly and rely on my brain and what moral courage I had to see me through.

'Leave me alone, leave me alone,' I demand violently, aware that I am shouting in both English and Portuguese, the official language of this newly independent state where I have been living for a decade. I've forgotten my Afrikaans after twenty years in exile, I'm screaming for my life yet with some control, some politeness, since after all I am a middle-aged lawyer in a public place.

'I would rather die here, leave me, I'd rather die here.'

I feel a sudden surge of elation and strength as I struggle, making an immense muscular effort to pull myself free. I might be an intellectual but at this critical moment without time to plan or think I am fighting bravely and with the courage of the youth of Soweto even though the only physical violence I have personally known in my life was as a schoolboy being tackled carrying a rugby ball. I hear voices coming from behind me, urgent, nervous voices not talking but issuing and accepting commands, and they are referring to me.

The darkness is total, but still I hear tense staccato speech.

'Lift him up, put him there.'

I am not a him, I am me, you cannot just cart me around like a suitcase. But I am unable to struggle any more, I just have to go along and accept what happens, my will has gone.

We are travelling fast, the way is bumpy, how can they leave me in such discomfort, if they are going to kidnap me at least they could use a vehicle with better springs. I have no volition, I cannot decide anything or even move any part of me. But I have awareness,

I think, therefore I am. The consciousness fades and returns, swirls away and comes back, I am lying down like a bundle, there is a point in my head that is thinking, and then oblivion and then awareness again, no thought related to action, but passive acknowledgement that my body is being transported somewhere, that I exist, even if without self-determination of any sort. I wonder if we have reached the South African border yet, I wonder who my captors are, what their faces look like, do they have names? This darkness is so confusing.

More urgent voices, speaking with rapid energy, treating me as an object, to be lifted and carried and moved this way and that . . . I feel the muscles and movements of people all around me, above me, at my side, behind me. Nobody engages me as a person, speaks with head directed towards me, communicates with me. I exist as a mass, I have physicality, but no personality, I am simply the object of other people's decision. They point their mouths to each other, never towards my head, I am totally present, the centre of all the energetic talking, but I am never included in the discussion, my will, my existence is being violated, I am banished even while in the group.

All is very still and calm and without movement or voices or muscular activity. I am wrapped in complete darkness and tranquillity. If I am dead I am not aware of it, if I am alive I am not aware of it, I have no awareness at all, not of myself, not of my surroundings, not of anyone or of anything.

'Albie . . .' through the darkness a voice, speaking not about me but to me, and using my name and without that terrible urgency of all those other voices '. . . Albie, this is Ivo Garrido speaking to you . . .' the voice is sympathetic and affectionate, I know Ivo, he is an outstanding young surgeon and a friend '. . . you are in the Maputo Central Hospital . . . your arm is in a lamentable condition . . .' he uses a delicate Portuguese word to describe my arm, how tactful the Mozambican culture is compared to the English one, I must ask him later what that word is '. . . we are going to operate and you must face the future with courage.'

A glow of joy of complete satisfaction and peace envelops me, I am in the hands of Frelimo, of the Mozambican Government, I am safe.

'What happened?' I am asking the question into the darkness, my will has been activated in response to hearing Ivo's voice, I have a social existence once more, I am an alive part of humanity.

A voice answers, close to my ears, I think it is a woman's, '. . . a car bomb . . .' and I drift back, smiling inside, into nothingness.

2

I am elsewhere and other. There is a cool crisp sheet on me, I am lying on a couch, aware that I have a body and that I can feel and think and even laugh to myself, and everything seems light and clean and I have a great sense of happiness and curiosity. This is the time to explore and rediscover myself. What has happened to me, what is left of me, what is the damage? I am feeling wonderful and thinking easily in word thoughts and not just sensations, but maybe there is internal destruction . . .

Let me see . . . A joke comes back to me, a Jewish joke from the days when we Jews still told jokes to ward off the pains of oppression and humiliation, from when I was still a young student and my mountain-climbing friend had a new joke for me each week, and I smile to myself as I tell myself the joke, and feel happy and alive because I am telling myself a joke, the one about Himie Cohen falling off a bus, and as he gets up he makes what appears to be a large sign of the cross over his body.

A friend is watching in astonishment. 'Himie,' he says, 'I didn't know you were a Catholic.'

'What do you mean, Catholic?' Himie answers. 'Spectacles . . . testicles . . . wallet and watch.'

My arm is free and mobile and ready to respond to my will. It is on the left side and I decide to alter the order a little, I am sure Himie would not mind in the circumstances. Testicles . . . My hand goes down. I am wearing nothing under the sheet, it is easy to feel my body. My penis is all there, my good old cock (I'm alone with myself and can say the word) that has involved me in so much happiness and so much despair and will no doubt lead me up hill and down dale in the future as well, and my balls, one, two, both in place, perhaps I should call them testes since I am in hospital. I bend my elbow, how lovely it is to be able to want again, and then be able to do what I want; I move my hand up my chest, what delicious self-determination, what a noble work of art is man . . . Wallet . . . My heart is there, the ribs over it seem intact, the blood will pump, the centre of my physical being, the part you take for granted is okay, I am fine, I will live and live robustly. Spectacles . . . I range my fingers over my forehead, and cannot feel any craters or jagged pieces, and I know I am thinking clearly, the darkness is now feather-light and clean, unlike the heavy, opaque

11

blackness of before. Watch . . . my hand creeps over my shoulder and slides down my upper arm, and suddenly there is nothing there . . . so I have lost an arm, Ivo did not say which one, or even that they were going to cut it off, though I suppose it was implicit in his words, and it's the right one, since it is my left arm that is doing all the feeling . . . So I have lost an arm, that's all, I've lost an arm, that's all. They tried to kill me, to extinguish me completely, but I have only lost an arm. Spectacles, testicles, wallet and watch. I joke, therefore I am.

3

So this is what it's like. I came close to death and survived. I am in the intensive care ward, there are tubes running into me like I've seen in the films and it always looked so uncomfortable, how could you bear to have a tube going into your nose or into your arm? And yet it is not difficult at all, the whole body feels slightly odd and the tubes are just part of the general strangeness. I know that time has passed, but have no sense of how long it has been; when you sleep, your body clock keeps going, but not when you are being operated on. Somebody told me that the operation lasted seven hours, that is how they measure ops, and I remember the sense of pride in his voice. They explored all of me, looking for damage everywhere, taking out scores of pieces of shrapnel from all over my body and head, and I was proud of my complicity in this major surgical enterprise.

And now, is it the same day or the next or the

next? The darkness has continued, and I suppose I am quite heavily drugged, and I just do not know how long I have been here. I remember Ivo talking to me once, chatting to me with the intimacy of a friend, re-establishing a personal relationship after having cut up my body, and giving me his personal version of the bomb story that has apparently stirred all Maputo, telling me he heard a tremendous explosion shortly after he had got up, and that he dressed quickly and rushed to the hospital without waiting to be called because he knew from the violence of the bang that there would be victims, and then when he got to the hospital he saw someone being carried in and looked closer and was shocked to see it was me in my bathing trunks. And then there was Anatoli, with the gentlest hands of any man I have known. I wonder what he looks like – from his name and the way he speaks Portuguese I guess that he is one of the Soviet doctors at the hospital – all I know is that he peels the bandages off with lovely delicacy, speaking softly as he dresses the wounds on my right side and then winding the bandages on again with equal fingerly kindness.

Someone has given me a rundown of my injuries: it seems there has been no injury to internal organs and no brain damage (I could have told them that, spectacles . . . testicles . . .) and that apart from the loss of the arm I have four broken ribs, a fractured heel on my right leg and a severed nerve in my left leg, lots of shrapnel wounds, ruptured eardrums and, as for my eyes, they would know as soon as they took the dressing off which would be quite soon, all in all a miracle, if you had seen my car, it is still there, everybody is driving past or walking by, and nobody believes I could have escaped alive, it is just a heap of crumpled metal with two beach chairs peeking out the back.

From time to time I allow the fingers of my left hand to trace the slope of my right shoulder. The whole of that side is heavily bandaged and I do not want to press too hard, but I can feel the shape of the upper part of the arm, and then before I can reach the elbow, the bandages turn inwards and there is nothing more. If I did not feel with my left hand, I would not know that I had lost my right arm, it still seems to be there, it exists in sensation even if not in reality. What puzzles me is something else, and the doctors do not seem to have an explanation for it, and that is, why, after having been through what must have been a terrible experience, and lying in complete darkness with a mass of fractures and wounds, I am feeling so wonderful.

4

Everybody is so kind, so gentle, so warm. The voices are friendly and supportive, telling me that they are about to remove the dressings from my eyes, would I lie still, please? By now I am used to fingers deftly placing and removing bandages. My contribution is simply to lie still, and I do it with all my heart and soul, there has never been a patient so good at lying still . . . I hear a murmur above me, from an unfamiliar voice, it is a woman speaking, and she is saying: first the right side . . . I feel the softness of the dressing being lifted, and there right above me filling the whole screen of what I can see – and I can see, I can see, as I knew I would be able to do – is the large, round, serious face of Dr Olga.

I get a slight shock seeing her there looking down on me, since only about ten days ago we had a small altercation when I went to the ophthalmic section of the hospital to get my eyes tested for reading glasses. There was an enormous crowd there, and nowhere to sit, and I tried to push my way forward, and she always sent me back, we were both tense with overwork, and now I want to apologize to her, but from the look of immense tenderness and concern she is giving me, it is not necessary.

Now the left eye, she says, and lifts the material from that side of my face. She covers my left eye, and I can see perfectly. She covers my right eye, and I can see nothing. So I have lost the sight of my left eye, but it does not seem to matter since I can see quite well with the other one. Dr Olga is speaking to me, she does not seem to be angry like the last time: We will put drops in the left eye and hopefully it will recover by itself, this is not the time to intervene. I smile and lift my left arm to take her hand in mine.

I have to twist my wrist to meet the palm of her right hand, I suppose all my handshakes will be a bit back to front from now on, but it is not difficult and more than made up for by the pleasure of being able to direct my movements and convey my own emotions to another human being.

Everybody around me is smiling, and I can feel that I have a great grin on my face, which must look funny in the midst of all my bandages. Some of the faces are new to me, some I recognize. Anatoli has dark hair and a soft face to go with his soft hands. He somehow looks more normal and less medical than I had imagined, and tells me that soon he will be replacing the dressings. A man introduces himself to me as a Captain of Security, and assures me that he or someone else will be there day and night to attend to any of my requests, and that there are many people who want to visit me and we should agree on the names . . . He is beaming, and speaks in a gentle way so as not to alarm me. The security aspect does not worry me at all, even though it should, considering that one of our guys was assassinated while in a hospital bed in nearby Lesotho, and another was almost certainly given poison while in this very hospital. I feel immune, I have survived the blast and they cannot get me now, it would be too obvious, too monstrous. I respond with equal warmth, wondering who the persons are who want to see me and if Lucia is among them, and how I would feel if I were to see her again.

5

I nearly died, I nearly died, but I did not. The movies get it all wrong, they always try to show the approach of death through visual imagery, when the visual world is the first to go and the last to come back, and what I had was an entering and receding aural and emotional universe, a tiny and insecure point of perception in my head, a flickering fragment of ego, and a certain awareness of sensationless mass. There was light darkness and heavy darkness and a complete oblivion that had no texture but was simply total. I could hear much of the time, able to pick up the emotional tone of the voices long after I had lost the significance of the words; perhaps it is true that deep meaning exists more on the emotional level than on the intellectual.

I resented being carried around like a sack of potatoes (in Mozambique a rare commodity, a sack of potatoes would have been well treated), it reminds me of what the kids used to say jokingly to me at school: Sachs, bags, bottles and rags. If the doctors ever want to know, I will tell them that it is important to speak warmly and calmly to the concussed patient, even if he or she appears to be unconscious, to give him or her orientations as to place and what is happening, and a sense of being supported and loved, if doctors are permitted to love. I wonder if my eyes were open, if I was speaking? I must ask somebody some day.

As children we used to have real, deep arguments, everything in the world depended on their outcome, did God exist and when you were on the point of dying did you have visions of the Lord or of heaven or hell, and did you begin praying in your last moments as great agnostics or non-believers were supposed to have done? Now I am lying peacefully in my bed, enjoying the chance to answer the questions that lay tucked away in my semi-consciousness all these decades, a little disappointed that the experience was in fact so banal. Perhaps you end up where you started off; if you believe, you can recall a sense that some guiding power was with you all the time, if you are a non-believer, you remember that there were no visions of the hereafter, no sense that you had a spirit apart from your body, there was no religious imagery or sensation at all. Somehow it no longer seems so vital to define oneself philosophically, there are believers who are simply pious and empty of any warm religiosity, and non-believers who have deeply spiritual natures . . .

I wonder where the idea comes from that as you are about to die your whole past life flashes by? There was nothing, absolutely nothing to suggest the faintest bit of instant retrospective, nothing to recall my childhood in a highly politicized, strongly anti-racist home, nothing about my days at the University of Cape Town in the mid-1950s, where first I discovered Lorca and Neruda and then the ANC, nothing about my years at the Bar, not even a flying gown or barking judge, nothing about the years in England and the happy days and the unbearably sad days of the marriage between Stephanie and me. Far from gaining memory, I lost it altogether, at least for the moments preceding the explosion; if they say it was a car bomb, naturally I believe them, but I cannot even remember going down from my apartment to the street, all I can recall was packing a picnic bag feeling sorry that it was only for one, and that it was a lovely late summer day and I was thinking of the beer I would have after my long slow jog on the beach.

One day I will think about Ruth, about our dear friend and comrade Ruth First, also a member of the ANC who had come to the university here, and the significance of the fact that the bomb that was sent to kill her succeeded while the bomb meant to kill me failed – if she were alive she would be the first to encourage me to go on living and not to dwell on her death – right now I hug my life around me and glory just in being. But curiosity is part of being, and one thing I thought about, virtually every day of my life since that terrible moment six years ago when she was blown up at her professorial desk not far from here, was whether, in the instant that the bomb went off, she realized what was happening. I think I know the answer now, and mercifully it is: no.

6

She is crooked in my arm, on my good side which is my left side, nestling so close that I cannot see her, only feel her, it could be anyone, no, not anyone, it must be a woman, I would not receive nor, I suppose, would I accept, this fleshly softness and intimacy from a man. Lucia. Her face looked strained and tense as she entered – I noticed she was wearing the lovely earrings she had had made with the stones I had given her – as though she had not slept, and I saw strands of grey in her long black hair. She put a carrier bag down near my bed, and I smiled, intensely happy at having the chance of sharing my joy at survival with someone from out there, coming from the world I used to inhabit, the wide universe of people and emotions and of activity that went beyond lying still, turning this way and opening my mouth. She brought in the feeling of that world, and would take out my feelings with her. Seeing my warm smile, she smiled back with the quick and intense smile that always flashed to her face when she was happy. Then, moving to my side, she grasped me with the spontaneity and courage that had captivated me when we were together.

I want to speak, I want to communicate, but above all I want to feel. Women are so much better than men when it comes to feelings. Men talk to you and smile and use words like brave and strong and the struggle, but after shaking my back-to-front hand and sensing relief that the introduction has been so easy, they sit back in their chairs and engage me with words. Women come forward, they hold your arm and nuzzle against your cheek, enabling you to crook your arm around their heads and stroke their hair and feel the tenderness in yourself coming out while you are receiving physical love and comfort from them. The doctors have done their bit, now what I need is endless stroking and warmth. It is a strange thing, I know that the attempt on me was totally impersonal, probably undertaken by someone who had never met me and who almost certainly had no feelings about me or animus towards me as a person, yet I feel as though a terrible hatred exists in the world against me, and in spite of the sense of triumph at having survived, I have an overwhelming and primitive need to be reassured of my worth as a person. I want to be cradled and fondled and loved, not hear how brave I have been or receive speeches however warm and comradely . . .

Lucia, Lucia, you came to be at my side, to help me, to comfort me with your shoulder and arms and face, to love me as a person even though your heart is with another. I want all the affection and love you can give me, to help me counteract the sense of being worthless, of being a piece of rubbish to be wiped from the face of the earth, of being destined for extermination. Whatever my rational self says, however great my feeling of happiness at my continued existence, a deep part of me has absorbed the aggression contained in the bomb, the shock to my being, the hatred of an intelligence seeking my destruction. Help me, help me – though I say nothing, it is my body that opens itself to receive your warmth – help me, help me, our love is over, but be with me now. No one will believe me that in terms of pure suffering, in terms of emotional pain, I grieved far more severely over the loss of your love than over the loss of my arm; as one of Tolstoy's characters once said, and perhaps the statement only seemed profound because I read it in Tolstoy: who knows the ways of the human heart? So, please, *mi amor*, my former love, let me continue to cradle your head, your hair, your cheeks, your neck, and may you carry on forever nuzzling and stroking wherever you find a bit of me not covered by bandages.

Pulling herself away, her hands gliding along and caressing my arm as she straightens up, she lifts the carrier bag near the foot of my bed, and takes out a little plastic box which I recognize as one of those we used to put salads in when we went to the beach together. Lucia enjoys practical things, the more emotional she is, the more she likes to involve herself in concrete arrangements. I am the opposite, the stronger my feelings at any moment, the more other-worldly I become. After prising the lid off, she shows me succulent little bites of marinated fillet steak, cooked with flair and richness, I have no doubt. She is a fine cook, and inspired me to cook well and love good eating – in fact this was the great revelation for me of our relationship, discovering pleasure in living, in enjoying beautiful things that had no purpose other than being beautiful, in buying silk and earrings and gold (no, I stopped at gold; even someone with the fanatic zeal for pleasure of a lapsed puritan has his outer limits); we spend half our lives trying to build habits of purity and self-denial, in which every tiny action is moralized, and then dedicate the other half to trying to de-moralize ourselves again. Being in the struggle and willing to give our lives surely does not mean that we must be style-less and dry and without passion for enjoyment.

Politically she was often more severe and unforgiving

than I was, but socially, during the years we lived together, she was much softer and more vivacious. Now, as my left arm holds her close to my bandaged shoulder, I feel my psyche liberated from all these ambiguities, I feel intuitively that all bad is attached to those who tried to kill me, and all good to my doctors, my nurses, the security team, my comrades, my friends, my family, Lucia and, of course, myself. Perhaps that is why I have this continuing feeling of elation; after a lifetime of striving, of feeling inside myself that everything, work, love, the struggle, family relationships, even pleasure, is locked in contradiction, suddenly the world is totally without paradox and dilemma, and my personal itinerary is clear and open and free of emotional stress; they tried to kill me and they failed, that's all that matters, and all I have to do is get better, that is my single, lovely, clean, political, public, and intimate goal.

'I can't,' I say, looking at the little pieces of meat for which I have no appetite.

She looks startled.

'It's too rich for me.'

She was offering something special, a delicacy she was sure I would appreciate. We are shouting a little, my hearing has been affected, and I sense that my voice is coming out like a command when all I want to do is talk gently.

'A soft-boiled egg, three and a half minutes, and some lemongrass tea, that's what I want.'

She laughs, and kneels just behind me and I realize she is going to kiss me. It cannot be on my lips, that would be too sexual, it can't be on my nose, that would be too ridiculous, but the rest of me is covered in bandages. She brings her mouth forward and deftly places it where there is just a little patch of bare skin on my neck. I feel the soft and pleasurable pressure of her lips, after all this time.

'And here we were thinking you were dead,' she murmurs.

7

No one seems to know what to do. The newspeople, normally so full of questions, are quiet; they seem shocked by my appearance, I do not know whether it is the short, tightly bandaged arm, or the shaven head or even seeing me in pyjamas, which affects them – Mozambicans are very conscious of dress, and Professor Albie should at least be in a safari suit.

The hospital room is crowded with TV cameras and journalists, and I am lying back, with my face and body swathed in clean white bandages. The journalists are waiting for me to speak, I am expecting them to fire away. Standing at my side are my children, Alan and Michael, in their late teens and seeming enormously tall as I look upwards towards them. I wonder what it was like for them in London to receive the news, to hear that their father had been blown up by a bomb. What did they tell their friends, was it on the news? It was a lovely moment when, sent by the ANC to be with me, they walked quietly into the hospital room, put their arms around me and said: 'Hi, Dad, how are you feeling?' In a way I feel it is premature for them to be protecting and comforting me, I am not old enough, but the naturalness and ease of their love was beautiful. 'Mom sends her love.'

People either smile when they are in my presence, normally in response to my smile, or else have grim and heavy faces, especially those who know me. I cannot stand the sad looks, they weigh me down, I want visitors to enter my cheerfulness and I am forced to spend a little emotional effort each time to break the mood. Now there are twenty journalists standing around in clumps, and it is not easy to establish the warm and optimistic mood I want. Someone has to create the conditions whereby the intense emotion in the room is converted into dialogue and into good television.

'I am leaving for London this evening to continue my medical treatment there.'

I open the interview, speaking with the deliberate emphasis that always comes into my voice when I know it is being recorded. The lights are in the wrong position, and I suggest that they be moved, and that the cameras be placed a little more to the side.

This session with the journalists was my idea; after a decade in Mozambique, having lived through the marvellous popular upsurge and excitement of the first years of independence, and then the hard recent period of setbacks and suffering, I do not wish to be carried out of the country clandestinely on a stretcher.

'The whole of Maputo heard the explosion, with the exception of one person. Do you know who that was?' I ask, aware that I am shouting a little and exaggerating my South African accent and the slightly patronizing tone that I have difficulty in controlling.

The journalists look puzzled.

'Me,' I answer.

I go on to explain my struggle while blinded by concussion, when I thought I was being kidnapped, and then give in detail the story of hearing Ivo's voice telling me I was in hospital . . . 'And I felt a great surge of elation when I heard these words, because I knew I was in the hands of Frelimo.'

The journalists are filming and writing energetically, and I sense that they are moved by this last statement, as I am, because it is true and conveys something of the emotion I have felt these past ten days in hospital, when I have had the sensation that the whole city has been cheering me on. It has been like a passionate cantata, a reaffirmation through the episode of the bomb and my survival of the simple indignation and fervour of the early years of the Revolution. It is not just the number of people who penetrated the security to see me, but the intensity of their feeling, the rich expressiveness of their emotion.

There are two people I specially hope will see the interview on TV, two very special visitors. The first was someone I had loved fervently, obsessively and not always happily when I first came to Mozambique, long before I met Lucia, and when my marriage to Stephanie was finally coming to an end. How much it meant to me now to have her by my side even if just for a few moments reviving the subliminal memories of our earlier physicality, all the stress gone, just the semi-conscious but intense recall of our coupling and kissing – I wished to summon up all the women I had held in my arms in all my life to rescue me with unstated remembrance of instinctual physical contact, with healing reminders that once upon a time my body and person had been lovable and loved, I wanted to call up carnal magic to counteract the traumatic spell imposed on me by my enemies. The other, whose visit surprised me by the impact it had on me, was my upstairs neighbour; for years I have wondered how my neighbours felt about having an ANC person in their midst, with the ever-present possibility of an attack on the premises, even though I never thought I would be a target because it was well known that I was not engaged in any kind of military or underground work – my neighbour, who had always been correct and a bit distant, now took my hand and pressed it to her breast, and said that the whole building had wanted her to come and see me and convey their anger and solidarity and desire for me to make the speediest possible recovery.

I tell the journalists the joke about Himie Cohen falling off the bus, but is is a mistake, jokes do not translate easily. They look at me as though the bomb has affected my head a little, and I try to recover by saying how much my years in Mozambique have meant to me.

I am excited, more than a little high. I sense that there are filmic and human interest aspects that are not being taken advantage of, and suggest they ask my brother, who is a doctor working at a well-known hospital in London, what he thinks of the treatment I have been receiving. Johnny, also sent out by the ANC, slightly younger than myself, we are very, very close, we always support each other, yet we articulate little. I beckon him to my side . . . He is the perfect person to have with me at this moment, able to help me take decisions about my immediate future and then to be my escort and companion in carrying them out. Twenty-five years earlier, when he was undergoing open-heart surgery and I was in jail, we had joked ruefully about our poor mother, her son the doctor in hospital and her son the lawyer in prison. Now the son the lawyer is in hospital, and the son the doctor is at his side, praising the Mozambican doctors for their excellent treatment.

Next I suggest that my children be asked a few questions, I cannot understand why the journalists did not think of it themselves, it was not my intention, but I seem more and more to be taking over the interview and directing the filming from my hospital bed. First Alan speaks, his London accent and style contrasting strongly with my South African one, then Michael. It is not just a question of accent, but of speaking style and intonation, even of body posture. It is a source of sadness to me that they have never been to South Africa and seen the country where Stephanie and I came from, the country where the ANC was born, the country of our passion and destiny, but I accept their right to be and feel themselves English, and am proud that they can speak well as they are doing in front of the cameras.

'Gita,' I say, 'come and sit next to me and say a few words.'

Gita is my friend, my colleague, my co-author and my boss. When I first arrived in Maputo to give lectures in the newly opened Law Faculty of the university, her husband acted as my Portuguese interpreter, and the three of us have been close friends ever since. Later when I moved to become director of research in the Ministry of Justice, she was my immediate superior, and we did everything together – workshops on maritime law, authors' rights, transfer of technology, women's rights, community courts, research on family law, building up a modern law library, editing a journal, publishing books and statutes. She is witty, a great conversationalist and talker, she knows this city inside out, the ways of doing things, the nuances of culture and style. In front of the camera she does not hug me or stroke my arm or show any sisterly emotion. I take her hand in mine and close my fingers around hers as she begins to talk, sensing that I am imposing intimacy on her, aware of a slight culture clash. Something which I find strange has been happening over the years in Mozambique – the more intense the emotion, the more the public restraint; even during the terrible hours when the news came through of President Samora's tragic and possibly provoked death in a plane crash, the anguish only came out in private tears.

My last day in Maputo, one that I want to be special and memorable, I wish everybody in the room to be as madly ebullient as I am, but the emotions are the wrong way round, as though, shocked by my appearance, the journalists are the injured ones, while, elated at being alive, I am the one who is whole. At the airport it should be better, my close colleagues from work will be there and we can make it a really joyous and celebratory farewell.

'I will be back,' I declare, as the interview comes to an end. Yes, I say to myself, I will be back, and I will complete my run on the beach, I feel it inside me, I will be back, and nothing will stop me this time.

8

The ambulance is old and not very well sprung, and bounces quite a bit as it speeds to the airport, evoking faint reminders of my terrible and strange journey ten days ago. This time, however, I am conscious, and somewhat aware of pain, no, not so much of pain as of a generalized discomfort and unease in my body, intensified by the jolts of the racing vehicle. I wish I could see outside the walls of the ambulance and refresh my world of visual memory with views of the flowering trees that I know grace the avenues along which we are bumping; I know too that the gleaming white and summery high-rise buildings are out there, with the ocean in the background, that we should be passing the elegant grounds of the Polana Hotel, speeding by the university where Ruth was killed, racing past the small reed and zinc houses of Polana neighbourhood that includes the court where we filmed a story for the BBC, turning left through a factory district, passing the huge curving murals in Heroes Square that we photographed for the favourite of all my books, *Images of a Revolution*, and then rushing directly to the airport – if only they could put one-way mirrors into ambulances so that we could see out without ourselves being seen. The ambulance stops, starts, and stops again. We must be nearly there, but we could be anywhere; all I see still are the small confines around me.

I hear sounds outside. We have come to a halt, and the door at the back is being opened. I raise myself to greet whoever it is and prepare to be wheeled out. It is Gita, and she is harassed, stooping down under the ceiling of the ambulance as she approaches.

'Come this way,' she says to someone behind her.

I notice that it is dark outside, and that there are many people waiting to clamber into the ambulance. Turning to me, she apologizes for the confusion but says we are so late that there isn't time for me to be taken to the VIP lounge, and my colleagues will see me in the ambulance. Judges, prosecutors, law professors, file one by one into the ambulance, shuffle past me in an uncomfortable stoop, proffer me a handshake, and file out again. Everyone is in a hurry, no one smiles.

'Amancio!' I shout as one of my closest co-workers comes past me. I grab hold of his hand and try to keep him at my side for a moment so that we can have a quick farewell embrace, but the queue is pushing him along and all he can do is look startled. I had in mind a short spell with my closest colleagues from work, those with whom I had shared the miseries and excitements of day-to-day activity, a chance to say a few words, to smile and be happy and then to embrace each one of them. Instead it is a procession filing past as we filed past so many coffins of the fallen; my function is to be the corpse. There is no joy, only a terrible solemnity that depresses me ever more profoundly. And it is not my colleagues from work who are coming, the typists, the machine operator, the messengers and clerks with whom I have worked so immediately for so many years, with whom I have lost my temper at times, and they with me – and how liberating it was to be in a country where you could shout and be shouted at without feeling any racist dimensions – but more distant friends occupying senior positions in the Justice sector, who have dressed up smartly for the occasion. I wonder if they received formal printed cards with gold lettering '. . . has the honour to invite your Excellency and spouse to be at Mavalane Airport on the occasion of the departure of Albie Sachs . . .'

I am wheeled out of the back of the ambulance and on to the tarmac of the airport. It is strange and pleasant to be in the open night air. The sky is dark, but the airport building is lit by bright spotlights, and I can see the Mozambican airline aeroplane looming up only yards away. Two nurses grip the stretcher on which I am lying, lift it up and start carrying me up the steps into the plane.

I look towards the airport buildings and can dimly make out the visitors' balcony against the glare of the lights. We are half-way up the steps and soon my little journey in the fresh air will be over, and I will be in the enclosed space of the plane. A soldier stands nearby with his AK gun, the first thing I saw when I landed in Maputo ten years ago; it was a real person, not a poster – I wanted to dance and cry, and the word that came to my lips (though of course I did not say anything, just checked my baggage) was: Victory. How rarely could we say that, how many times had African people been trampled underfoot because of inferior firepower. Now I have seen so many guns, the war has dragged on for so long, so many problems have beset the army, that I no longer enthuse over the uniform or the arms in the same way, but something of that initial respect will always remain. Farewell, Mozambique, I am being carried away from you, who knows when I will return. So much has happened to your country and to me in these years, I am about to enter the plane, let me say goodbye.

I raise my head a little, lift my left arm in a final farewell and wave towards the balcony. The air is warm and the lights are confusing. Suddenly, amazingly and beautifully, there are hundreds and hundreds of arms waving back to me, and I feel the cantata of love and affection swelling out towards me again. The people of this city and I are in joyous, spontaneous communion, my friends, my colleagues are there, but also hundreds of strangers, it is a beautiful hallucination, as I raise my arm in a last farewell from my mummy-like body, all those arms swaying and rolling against the glare of the lights.

The nurses pause at the top of the staircase . . . *khanimambo*, Maputo, thank you, until we meet again . . . and then carry me into the plane.

TWO

9

I do not know why it is called a commode, there is nothing commodious about it, and what I am sitting on is nothing more than a little toilet on wheels. But I accommodate myself on it as though I am on a throne. I am independent of my bed, and despite the general feeling of having-come-down-to-earth since my arrival at this well-known London hospital (that in my case prefers not to reveal its name), I feel quite excited, in fact on the verge of a breakthrough.

This is not the first time I have sat on the commode. The process is quite cumbersome – I ring the little brass bell that rests next to the flowers and fruit on the stand at the side of my bed, ask the nurse if she would mind bringing the commode, and then when she wheels it in, wriggle my backside along the mattress and, steadying myself with my left arm, heave my body on to the seat. It is a small act, but I do it without help, in fact refuse assistance even at the risk of the nurses remarking with ambiguous praise that I am fiercely independent. For some reason, each time I battle to move my body on to the commode, a saying of Samora's comes to me: the success of the Revolution depends on the tiny daily acts of each one of us.

Is this what the Revolution has come to mean to me, is this what is left of that once glorious process that inspired me for so many years? Yet my duty, to myself, to those who love me, to all the comrades, is to get better, and that does not simply mean to make myself as physically whole as possible, but to emerge radiantly and forcefully and happily from the blast. And that means attending with as much enthusiasm as I can to the details of normalizing my life, like getting on to the commode. Judging from the letters I receive and from what some of my visitors say there are those who think I am a hero because of the way I came through the explosion, and this is something I am going to have to handle, and it will not be easy, but what I want to say to them is that there was no heroism in getting through the blast, I survived and that was a fact, there was virtually no choice or volition involved. What is far more heroic is this totally unheroic act of pulling myself across the bed and then defying the risk involved in the topple on to this commode.

At the same time, I must say it is fun. Every day there is a new discovery, a new accomplishment. Now I am perched on the commode with my glasses on my nose, a detective story in my hand, a roll of toilet paper nearby, and the bell within easy reach. And the drain. The drain is a nuisance, the piece of purgatory that accompanies me day and night, in my bed and out. It was the physiotherapist, not the doctors, who discovered that something was wrong. I said I was tired all the time and felt breathless after moving, and she suggested an X-ray and it was found that my right lung was collapsed. So now I have a tube running from the lung through my ribcage at the back – it was an unpleasant moment when they manoeuvred the little plastic pipe into my body – down to a bottle on the ground. Apparently the sac around the lung was punctured and is now full of bloody fluid which has to drain off slowly. The drain goes to sleep with me at night and wakes up with me in the morning and it accompanies me to the toilet.

This is the second time I am trying. On the other occasion I sat for half an hour anxiously hoping for an outcome. At times I consciously urged my bowels on, moralizing, telling little stories to the sphincters, pleading nicely, joking, getting cross and giving a big push, but nothing happened. All right, I said, let it mature, it is no good forcing the issue. And I concentrated on my book, losing myself as much as possible in the banter between Archie Goodwin and his corpulent, orchid-growing detective boss Nero Wolfe. *Murder by the Book*, one of Rex Stout's best stories; I wonder if it will always be a laxative for me. Three murders later, and there was still no movement of my bowels, though I must admit that I enjoyed the feeling of having a book in my hands again and being involved in a good read.

This question of heroism bothers me quite a lot. I am going to recover physically, but there are two things I am going to have to find a way of living with – the fact that I have lost an arm forever, and the fact that people regard me as something extraordinary, sometimes even as a hero. The arm part I will deal with step by step, starting with a prosthesis and becoming as self-sufficient as possible as quickly as I can manage. The being extraordinary part is much more difficult. I enjoy the praise, in fact I am proud myself that at least in my own mind I fought energetically at the crucial moments, but for the rest I did not do anything, just smiled with pleasure at being alive, which can hardly be regarded as being brave. I want to maintain my mood of elation as much as possible, but I hope that one day I can return to a normal life, whatever that means, without every action or word of mine being judged against the background of the bomb blast. I know that it is really up to me and how I behave, the question is: how should I behave?

These musings seem at least to be doing my intestines some good. There are promising little stirrings down there and I can feel the muscles beginning to move on their own and a tiny bit of substance starting to enter the passage. The movement continues, it is coming, it is coming. The substance extrudes itself, there is a tiny plop into the commode, and it is done. What relief, what a sense of joy and achievement. I shit, therefore I am. Shitting might be the most banal of activities, until your body is unable to do it. I feel somehow proud of my body, that part there inside that functions silently all the time without praise or even acknowledgement and only gets noticed when something goes wrong, and then it is cursed – who ever feels pleased with his or her digestive system, or shows it off or says it is brave? Now it is fighting back on my behalf, restoring me to health and normality. I lean forward and pick up the roll of toilet paper, prelude to another little encounter between me and the physical world. After all that has happened to me, after all the surgery and the nursing, after all the newspaper and TV stories, can I wipe my bum? It is not just a question of lavatory humour, a little joke I have with myself at the moment, this is the actual frontier of struggle. I put the roll between my knees, unwind a short length and pull. The paper does not break, and I begin to feel uneasy, almost panicky. It will be terrible if I cannot even tear off some toilet paper. I must steady myself, hold the roll carefully and at the right angle, and tug again. One, two, three . . . It works. I have a piece of toilet paper ready, and now another and yet another. Now for the difficult part, getting it to my behind with my left hand, I am not used to it, some people say that in certain cultures you always wipe your ass with your left hand because your right one is for shaking hands, but that was never a prescription of my culture. I lean forward, raise part of my backside, slip my hand in and begin to wipe. Victory.

I reach for the little bell and give it a few triumphant tinkles.

10

This is the hardest moment, waking in the early hours of the morning and finding the same repetitive words of the song jumping unbidden and unwelcome into my head: It's me, it's me, o Lord . . . I cannot stop the refrain . . . It's me, it's me o Lord . . . The words repeat themselves in my skull . . . It's me, it's me o Lord. Half awake, half asleep, I have no defences, no active personality at this hour. It is neither light nor dark outside and I pull my blankets over me to get another hour's sleep. This is the time when I am most alone and most aware of my situation. If I lie still, my body feels stiff. If I roll over to the side, which requires much heaving and pulling, all sorts of pains enter my bones, I feel clumsy, my joints are out of articulation, my body is distorted.

During the day I hardly feel pain. My whole body is sore and I am uncomfortable all over, with a vague generalized sense of aching. But it is nothing like that sharp, biting, intolerable hurting of earache or root-canal treatment. There are certain parts of my body that are still severely wounded and tender, and twice I have really felt sore, the first being when the ear specialist in Maputo washed out my shattered eardrum with a syringe – I cried out, and almost hit him – the second when the drain was plunged through my ribcage, though the latter was more a miserable sensation of my flesh being torn than actual consciousness of pain. But on the whole, during the day when I am active and alive, my physical suffering seems surprisingly light. Evenings are also not too difficult. The harsh moments are at this hour when I feel myself to be naked and fully exposed to the effects of the blast.

My scalp feels as though it is tightly drawn over my head, pressing down like a clamp on my cranium. Having a blind eye strengthens the feeling of strangeness. It is not that I notice that I am partly blind, but there is a kind of heaviness at that side, as though my head is being weighed down. Then the whole of my right side seems to be broken and full of wounds, all the way down to my pulverized heel. They say the ribs are knitting well and that the holes and cuts are clean and are gradually healing. But it almost feels that the top right-hand portion of my body is not part of me, but rather something that I am clutching to my side to keep under my protection . . .

It's me, it's me o Lord . . . Everything will get better, but I will never recover my arm, it will not grow or be there again, there will always be an empty space where my arm should be. Albie for the rest of his life will be without his right arm. It did not happen to someone else, this is not something I am experiencing through another, hearing about it, in a book or a film. It's not my brother nor my sister, but it's me o Lord . . . The spiritual is personal and intimate and laden with a sad and inescapable sense of destiny. During the day when I am being looked after by the nurses or when visitors come, I can feel excited. Now I am in solitude, confronted by my body without comfort, distraction or fantasy, and deeply aware that my physical self has been mutilated, for ever. This short protuberance wrapped in bandages that extends from my shoulder is all that is left of what I once took for granted as my arm. When it was there I never thought about it, it was simply there. Now that it is gone I notice the space where it used to be.

I lost my arm, my watch, my signature, my hand-shake, the callous on my middle finger where I held my pen and of which I was so proud, my only answer to the callouses on the hands of workers. All is confused on that side. I sense that my fingers are still there, I can feel them vividly, usually tingling and clenched, though I know that it is all imagination, phantom limb, as they say.

Occasionally the thought flashes through my mind that the doctors or someone must have done something with my shattered arm after severing it, perhaps they burnt it, I cannot imagine what else you do with an amputated arm, but that does not matter, by then it was no longer my arm, the limb that had protected me and saved me and given itself so that the rest of me might live; the arm that I love so much now that it is posthumous, was destroyed by the would-be assassins, not by the doctors.

I lie in the gradually lightening darkness talking to myself without moving my lips, aware that there are some things so intimately involved with your body that you cannot escape them, they are there inside you, part of you, aspects of your innermost existence where your body, mind and personality meet and interact without subterfuge or strategy. I would not

41

say that these repeated nocturnal moments of bleak self-confrontation are more real than the hours of vivid activity during the day, but nor can I affirm that they are less real. I am one person, not two, and all I can hope is that the lively daytime Albie can help heal and restore confidence to the traumatized and lonely Albie of the early hours.

My neck is sore, the back of my head is tender. I puff the pillows as much as I can and try to drift off to sleep.

It's not my brother, nor my sister, but it's me o Lord, standing in the need of prayer . . . it's not my uncle nor my cousin but it's me o Lord, standing in the need of prayer . . .

11

The sibilant roar of approaching car wheels on the damp road surface seems abnormally dissonant and menacing. Eddie the porter is manoeuvring me with grace and courtesy in a wheelchair towards the main building where I am going for an X-ray. My head seems to pick up all sound indiscriminately and without meaning, perhaps my eardrums are still ruptured and making me feel a bit idiotic. I hate the moment when we leave the pavement to cross the road, I feel completely unprotected and I am angry at the thought that if a car bears down on me there is nothing I can do, that my body and my survival are totally in the hands of another. My volition counts for nothing; after all that has happened, to die a banal death run over by a car would be intolerable.

Luckily Eddie has a good touch and is in rapport with me and the wheelchair, he can do a neat right-about turn, an elegant wheel-chair hop up on to the pavement, and, most difficult of all, a nifty swish through heavy swing doors. Please, please Eddie why are we going so slowly across the road?

At last we reach the other pavement. Now I can stare up at the passers-by. This is the fun part of the journey, the bit that sets my thoughts sprinting. You, sir, walking past, noticing me but not wanting to stare, yes you – I say to myself – all you see is a figure huddled in a blanket being wheeled along the street, a pair of expressionless eyes looking vaguely in your direction, feet pressed on the little flaps at the bottom of the chair. You feel faintly sorry for that creature you are passing and a sense of mild embarrassment mingled with relief that it is not you. Do not worry, sir, I know exactly how you feel (or fail to feel) because until recently I was exactly like you and I must have passed hundreds of persons in wheelchairs in my time, and had just your feelings (or lack of feelings). And the fact of the matter is that I am alive and well and full of thoughts and feelings, and one of my thoughts right now is how wonderful it is to see you striding freely down the street, your knees bending and straightening in that extraordinary way that human limbs have evolved over the millennia, your body miraculously upright, your arms swinging just a little. Walking is poetry, enjoy it as such, sir, it is not simply a means of getting from point A to point B.

And you, madam, striding past with such energy, your shoes clopping so emphatically on the pavement, I do not mind if you look at me as you surge along and wonder about me and why I am in a wheelchair, it would not be an invasion of my privacy, in fact I do not want to be ignored, what I would like above all is that you notice me and think of me as just another person in the world going about his or her business, in this case the business of getting better. It so happens, madam, that this bundle you are rushing by has quite a story to tell, and it is not a sad one at all, and that it is full of laughs and has at least some personality. I do not know how you would call me, temporarily or permanently handicapped or disabled or whatever the terminology is today, but I am okay, there's a me that is intact and full of curiosity and fun, and all these attributes are contained in that apparently lifeless and dummy-like object with eyes that is fast disappearing from your sight. In a few moments the scientists are going to be looking at me, but I will also be scrutinizing them, seeing how they organize a hospital and what their techniques and styles of work are, because, madam, even if I appear completely immobile and passive, I am as active a part of the scene as you are.

The cool air brushes my face, I am shivering slightly, and am physically uncomfortable with the cold, but delighted to feel wind on my cheeks. I cannot gauge movement very well, people seem suddenly to appear and disappear, cars materialize from nowhere and then vanish. The angles are all wrong, the conjunctions of motion and space in disharmony, everything seems unusually big and to loom above me. Much as I am enjoying being in the open air, in confrontation with the traffic and with the public, I am also deeply disconcerted and alarmed, and it is with a sense of relief that I realize that Eddie is at last wheeling me imperiously through gaping automatic doors into the safe vestibule of the main hospital.

44

12

Her fingers are soft and gentle, and I cannot tell her how much my body responds to her touch. Carefully she unwraps the bandage that winds round and round my chest and shoulders, and then prepares to remove the gauze that lies on the wounds. The sterile equipment stands neatly arranged on the table, unwrapped from the sterile package – unlike Maputo where they had to boil and sterilize the instruments and the gauze each day. Disposable gloves, disposable tweezers and scissors, disposable bandages and disposable gauze, all that remains behind here after use is the nurse herself. The tweezers grasp the gauze and lift it with a soft movement, leaving my chest completely exposed. I always give a quick glance at the underside of the material to see how the blood and pus look, and to discover the places where the discharge is most evident. By now I can detect slight changes in colouration and texture but do not know how to interpret them. This is my first time in a hospital, and what a first time it is.

'Ooh, lovely,' she says, 'the wounds are coming along beautifully.'

I do not know how to judge, all I am aware of is that my body is a mass of scars and stitches and gaping cuts, and that a faint odour that I detest comes from the region around my armpit. The nurse dips a piece of sterile cotton wool in a sterile plastic cup containing sterile salt water, and begins bathing my wounds. It seems that in Maputo the bacteria are still underdeveloped and that if you get an infection you can still knock it out with antibiotics, while here in the developed world the bacteria are often so advanced that they resist all medication.

She has started at the back and is now bathing the injured part near my armpit. There is something infinitely lovely in the way she cleans the wounds, a delicacy and tenderness that is immensely kind to my body. I am not used to being stroked like this. As seems to happen these days, her movements evoke subliminal memories, this time of infancy, faint but deep remembrances of supportive arms, gentle hands, friendly fingers, loving touches. We are so eager and happy to leave our childhood behind us, and yet what a terrible loss we suffer without even thinking about it when we habituate ourselves to living without physical kindness. Stroking and caresses for adults are inter-mittent and exclusively related to love-making and sexuality. Apart from the occasional hug or the cour-tesy kiss, we have virtually no tender physical contact at all. For a woman to run her fingers down my body would be a sexual advance, for me to stroke her would be equally challenging and erotic. These little daily acts of physical appreciation and comfort, so natural towards infants, become highly charged and complicated when you are adult; what a terrible deprivation we impose on ourselves, and yet outside of the legitimacy established by love-making or healing we have no chance at all of recapturing tactile tenderness. I wonder if the nurse realizes that my body adores her, not in a sexual way, but unconditionally and openheartedly? Perhaps it is better that she does not know.

I see England through the prism of the nurses' fingers. My friends expect me to say that in the ten years of my absence, this country has become harder and less caring

46

and completely driven by the quest for money. But I cannot say that, even though from what I hear I believe it to be true. My own experience now is of infinite care and support, I am full of love for the English people because of these fingers that bathe me and clean me and bind my wounds each day, that is the reality of my experience.

There is a film on television evoking great controversy, about a British soldier seriously injured in the Falklands/Malvinas war with Argentina. I cannot bear to watch or even hear the explosions, or see pictures of the hero of the story in hospital. It is as though I have no emotion to spare for anybody but myself. In any event, the controversy is about whether he received adequate medical attention and support once the war was over and the heroism was forgotten, and I find it deeply paradoxical that his experience should have been so bitter while mine is so sweet.

I have always felt I would rather be sick in England than anywhere else (and rather die in any other country, English funerals being, if I might put it that way, so dead). But that was because I liked the manner in which the National Health Service was organized, as well as the modern non-interventionist approach to treatment. What I did not expect was the tenderness and emotional warmth of the nurses. I am receiving no antibiotics, no creams, no pills or injections to help deal with the wounds, just loving treatment from the nurses to encourage my body to heal itself.

There are only two activities they do not seem to like. One is shaving my face. They are so courageous and deft at handling my body that I am amazed at their timidity when it comes to passing the razor over my cheeks and chin. Perhaps shaving one's face seems to be a purely masculine activity, the sort of thing one can never learn in a nurses' training school. In fact I always shave myself, and notice their relief when I take the razor away. The other thing that irritates them, but I do not know what I can do about it, is picking up newspapers from the floor. When I can no longer read newspapers, I know I am dead. I get three every day, or, as they say here, I 'take' *The Times*, the *Guardian* and the *Independent*. Many of my friends have difficulty in choosing, but I am finding that one of them is emerging as my clear favourite, the *Independent* – it is the easiest of the three to fold with one hand. What happens is that I cannot control the pages easily, and discover that I have to throw them on the floor in sections when I have finished reading them.

The nurses do everything for me with genuine cheerfulness, except pick up the newspapers. They clean out my commode, take my bottle away when I ring for them in the middle of the night, take my temperature, my pulse, my blood pressure, bring my food and newspapers, dress my wounds, give me painkillers and sleeping tablets, and look after me with unstinting concern for my recovery. It is as total an experience as being in jail was, only completely the other way round, as fully dedicated towards my recuperation as prison was to my destruction.

The saline swab is now being carefully dabbed in the wounds on my chest. Perhaps because nurses spend three-quarters of their time doing what really is little more than housework for the patient, when it comes to actual nursing they put all their skill and feeling into it. Ouch! There is something tender at the point where she is cleaning. 'That was sore,' I tell her, sorry my reverie has been disturbed.

She looks down carefully and moves the cottonwool along the length of the wound.

'There's something in there, I can feel it,' she answers.

She pushes the swab backwards and forwards, from side to side. 'Oou, oou, oou,' I grunt, feeling prickles of pain with each movement. I have discovered that it is much better to let out some kind of sound when it hurts than to be stoical.

'Let me get the tweezers.' The nurse tears open a sterile paper bag, removes a pair of sterile plastic tweezers, and inserts them cautiously into the wound.

'Here we are,' she says with delight, and with a deft twist, lifts her hand and places the tweezers right in front of my face. It hurt as she pulled it out, but this time I do not groan, since I am fascinated to see what it is.

'Another piece of rubbish out,' she is triumphant.

'That's not rubbish,' I answer, 'that's my car.'

Caught between the ends of the tweezers is a flat jagged piece of dark material about the size of a little coin, the only relic I have of my lovely Honda. Shortly after I arrived here in London, the staff nurse took out my stitches, rows and rows of them, from my scalp and my back and my side and my stomach – after reaching fifty I stopped counting, feeling quite proud of the high number. Now a piece of shrapnel has worked its way out of its own accord. I must really be on the mend.

Round and round, the bandages are now being wound across my torso, the major work of the morning is complete. No two nurses tie bandages in exactly the same way, but all seem to get a special pleasure from the task and to have this same gentle and kindly touch. The bandages are more than a cover for the injuries, they are my dress, an integral part of my present personality. They not only keep the germs out, they keep me in; they are the reminders of the care and affection I am receiving from the nurses. I had that same feeling of unlimited satisfaction and gratitude when Anatoli changed my dressings in Maputo; there is much organized hate in the world, but also much organized love.

I enjoy being babied as an adult, and only wish that when one day I leave the hospital, this intimate physical affection will never end.

13

'Tell me, Margit, how did it happen?'

Margit looks a little startled, as if surprised that I who was at the scene, should be asking her, who was in Vienna, what happened. For the first time I feel I really want to know about the explosion. Until now I have refused to look at newspaper stories, and my visitors have had the tact not to raise the subject. I was not even curious. What was, was; what wasn't, wasn't. The important part was that I survived and now it was my job to get better.

It has been an emotional day. When Margit came in from the airport, she started to shake heavily, and I had to tell her to sit on the chair next to my bed, draw her to my side, hold her head in my arm and stroke her hair continuously, saying: it's all right, it's all right, it's all right. It took a long while and a lot of comforting on my part to get the trembling to subside, and my arm is still tingling with the effort, while she is still a bit shaken.

'Margit, I don't know what happened that day, tell me.'

I know I can trust her completely, that she will be as accurate as possible, leave out nothing relevant and add nothing for the sake of colour. We have been friends for many years. We argue about the politics of struggle, about women's rights, culture, films, music, whether the Left is in crisis or on the verge of immense renewal, even fashion. We know almost everything about each other's lives, and have frequently slept in each other's beds, though never at the same time. Perhaps that is the foundation of our friendship, the fact that we have an intimate, personal, relationship, with a vivid sense of maleness and femaleness, but without sex. We advise and counsel each other on our respective emotional lives without allowing the other to enter into the equation, not because either of us has not been free, but because that is just the way it has been. Sometimes I feel that love has nothing to do with destiny and everything to do with timing ('Every time I meet a really attractive woman, either she is married or I am married').

'What I am going to tell you is based on newspaper stories, letters and telephone calls.' Her voice is subdued but precise and I know I am going to get just the kind of concentrated factual report that I want. Nearly all my visitors start off by telling me how they heard the news, where they were standing at the precise moment ('It was like the Kennedy news,' one said). But this is the first time I am asking exactly what the news was they heard.

'It was about nine in the morning . . .' this I know '. . . and you were planning to go to the beach.' This I also know – and that the date was 7 April 1988.

'You went to your car which was parked just in front of your building, put something in the trunk, walked to the side in front where you placed a small bag . . .' that

51

would have been my chilled beer for drinking after my run '. . . and then went to open the door next to the driver's seat.'

'I have no memory at all of this,' I tell her, curious, baffled, excited and amused. 'And then . . .?'

'And then . . .' she is still grave 'and then . . . Sam Barnes your American friend drove past on the other side of the road with her baby in the back of her car and you looked up to wave to her . . .' This I have a dim and completely confused half-memory of, was it that day or some other time? '. . . and according to one version, that probably saved your life; there is some dispute over that.'

'And then . . .?' I am impatient.

'And then . . .' she pauses, there is a great intimacy between us at this moment. 'And then, the explosion took place, your car was thrown to one side and you were thrown to the other. I don't know if you saw pictures of your car.' I shake my head, I refused to look at the newspapers. 'It was crumpled up like a ball, and you were lying some distance away.'

'Was it remote control, or when I put my key into the door?'

'That we don't know. Some people came to pull you away in case there was another explosion. You were speaking to them, giving them instructions how to carry you . . .'

I smile and interrupt: 'You know what I thought? I thought it was agents of Pretoria . . .'

'Well, you spoke in English and Portuguese, and this was regarded as a good sign since if you were very deeply concussed you could only have spoken in your mother tongue.'

'Speak? I thought I was shouting, that I was fighting

52

for my life.' She still looks unusually quiet, while I am aware of a large grin on my face. This is one of the funniest stories I have ever heard: here was one of those crucial moments in your life where your physical bravery is put to the test, and you fight like hell, offering a heroic resistance, throwing your whole self into a massive do–or–die effort, and in reality all you are doing is to give a few feeble shrugs of your shoulders against people who are in fact trying to save you.

'The odd thing is that my body was right,' I continue. 'I was fighting for my life, all that adrenalin, preparing me for fight or flight, probably helped me survive.' I am always pleased in this anti–scientific age to discover that at least something I learnt in those days when we all believed in science is true.

Margit resumes her narrative. 'At that moment a team from the television studio nearby were setting out to make a film about Women's Day, and they pulled up their van and took you to hospital . . .' And that was when I thought I was being dragged over the South African border. The joke continues, no one can deny that life is crazy and amusing, the hospital was only a few hundred yards away.

Now it is my turn to enter the story. I tell Margit about hearing the surgeon's voice, and about Himie Cohen . . . spectacles . . . testicles . . . Margit and I may not be lovers but there is no harm in passing on some relevant information.

Under the influence of my animation, she is gradually becoming more confident, more like the Viennese jazz concert and rock group organizer I have known. I am so amused at the story of what really happened that I give her an extra few hugs and caresses. She responds by stroking my arm, placing my hand on her neck, pressing

53

her bosom against my shoulder, keeping up constant physical activity and friendly rubbing. I cannot receive too much affection, my body craves more stroking and more love. The doctors did a wonderful job in saving my life, but it is the kindness of the nurses and the love of my friends that is making me get well, of that I am sure, science or no science. There is something specific I think she can help me with.

'Margit, I've got a request for you.'

She looks expectant.

'You see these shortie pyjamas,' I continue, 'they are all I have in the world.'

She is puzzled.

'My suitcases never arrived from Maputo, so I not only lost my arm and my car and my job and my home and my country, I lost my clothing as well. I'm like a new-born baby, I start with nothing.'

She looks at me with sad and anxious eyes.

'It's terrific,' I say enthusiastically. 'I can re-create myself, it's a wonderful chance to start life all over again and I need a good producer to help me . . . how about it, Margit?'

For the first time she really smiles, she is beginning to enter into my excitement. That's what friends are for, not to help you with the banal things, but to encourage the absurdities that make you who you are. I explain to her that I have got a set of the brightest and most amusing shorts available in London, one with a tropical fruit design and two others with Charlie Chaplin all over them, while the top of me is covered with bandages, so the mode for hospital is colourful shorties, complemented by an attractive array of stylishly tied bandages.

'What I need is some lovely clothing for when I come

54

out of hospital, phase two of my recovery. And I know what I want, vivid and well-designed track-suits that I can feel nice in. I'll leave my other clothing till later.'

Margit is captivated with the idea of producing the new version of me, and says so. She knows just the shop, it's expensive . . . she looks up at me . . . but it's got beautiful stuff . . . I tell her that I haven't got very much money, but what I've got I want to spend on beautiful things. I find my feminist friends divide neatly into two classes, those who are anti-appearance and those who enjoy dressing attractively and with flair, and each goes the whole way. (Albie, why do feminists from England and the USA think it is good to look bad and bad to look good, I can't understand it? asked my friend from Italy, the only time she ever broke the ranks of sisterhood.) I can rely on Margit to choose clothes that are affirmative and witty; just as I did not want to creep out of Maputo, so I do not wish to sneak back into the world.

She is laughing now, and gives me a hearty kiss on my neck.

'I think that is a wonderful idea and I accept the role of producer.'

This is a little joke between us, since only a couple of weeks before the bomb she had been producing a video film with a Mozambican friend and myself on how the war in Mozambique was being reflected in the work of artists.

I absolutely must come to Vienna as soon as possible, she insists, they have good facilities for fitting prostheses there. (At least she does not tell me about the disabled people she knows who are so marvellous – I keep getting this from visitors, who have informed me about people with no legs at all who dance, with one leg who go skiing, with every kind of physical handicap who do every kind of wonderful activity. I do not like to hear about these people, partly because the underlying chain of thought is that when the speakers look at me they are seeing a man with a chopped-off arm, and partly because I become aware of a pressure to be wonderful like those persons talked about. I am sure all disabled people feel the same; at least six visitors have told me about someone they did not even know but only read about, an almost completely paralysed writer in Ireland who taps out his books with movements of his head.)

Time passes quickly, and Margit becomes more and more spirited, we joke and laugh together and make plans for completing the film and talk about my visit one day to Austria. When the moment arrives for her to leave we are both in such a glow that we forget completely the circumstances of the visit. We hug, kiss, stroke and embrace each other, and finally it is goodbye, full of laughter and jokes.

A few hours have passed, and I am feeling so anxious that I ring my little brass bell for the nurse and ask if, please, please, tonight or tomorrow or as soon as possible, could I see a psychiatrist?

14

Knock, knock. It is always the same, I wonder who it is, just as I used to wonder in prison, though there they never knocked. Sometimes I see the face in the little window panel in the door, but today it is closed.

Is it my friendly policeman?

Tall, well-built, polite, the sergeant from Scotland

Yard's Anti-Terrorist Squad drops in from time to time, to – as he puts it – liaise with me. I enjoy being liaised with, even if I am surprised that he comes by the Underground and not in a police car, and even if I get confused sometimes as to who the terrorists are and who the anti-terrorists and who the anti-anti-terrorists. I wonder on occasions what the sergeant really thinks of me; he is certainly most polite and correct, and never makes me feel that I am burdensome or antipathetic to him. How does he see the ANC, does he regard us as a bunch of terrorists with perhaps a few misguided folks like me in their ranks? (I cannot imagine that he actually thinks badly of me – in fact, in spite of the evidence of the bomb, I cannot imagine that anyone thinks badly of me.) And how do I see him?

To be honest, I am pleased that he comes, it gives me a certain sense of reassurance that the British Government is not going to stand by and watch me being bumped off, that they accept a certain responsibility. The Ambassador in Maputo came to see me at the hospital, insisted he had a right to see me 'as Albie's ambassador and his friend'. Is this part of a wider change in me, that I'm interested in clothes and ambassadors, and enjoy liaising with a gentleman from Scotland Yard? Or is it that we in the ANC are coming in from the cold and becoming part of the world? Or, more profoundly, is it that the world is changing, categories are becoming more fluid, struggles more complicated, alliances more elaborate? This is a strange time to think that struggle has become less simple, less direct, when I have just been a victim of an old-fashioned assassination attempt. Yet I feel convinced that one of the biggest tasks facing our movement at the moment is to overcome the psychology of the embattled and begin to think with the vision of leaders of the country as a whole. And yet, and yet, for all our new thinking, and breaking out of stereotypes, the police forces of the world continue their time-honoured surveillance and controls, and maybe I am just being naïve.

Perhaps part of my pleasure at being in this hospital room is that I am fairly sure it is not bugged. Sometimes I used to imagine my phone in Maputo being listened in to by at least three different secret services, and then get special satisfaction from encouraging Hungarian friends or those that spoke a little-known language from north-east India to make a call. A thought occurs to me: possibly my continuing sense of post-bomb euphoria comes from the fact that at least for the time being I am out of the net of hidden sensors, my spirit free from prying for the first time in three decades. Did the security police really follow every up and down of my marriage, pick up the terms of our divorce, record automatically the names of our children even before they were entered in the birth register?

I too have a dream, that there will one day be a world without police files, and bugged rooms, and tapped telephones, and intercepted mail, and that I will actually live in it. Ever since I was seventeen and became politically active, I have lived with the notion that there are others accompanying every move I make, listening to every word I say. How can you have an argument, express physical passion, write an intimate letter if you know that others might be listening in or looking on? My biography is there, little details and big events that I have long forgotten, recorded in the files of at least five countries, probably nearer twenty. One day I look forward to examining the biggest one of all, that of SACHS, ALBERT LOUIS (aka ALBIE) at Security

Headquarters in Pretoria. This is the Book that records implacably all the events of my life, that should decide whether I go to heaven or hell. Once when the Minister of Justice gave reasons for placing me under a banning order, he quoted from speeches I had made some years earlier, and I had forgotten them completely, and was delighted to rediscover my earlier moral earnestness and neat turn of phrase. Presumably it now has new entries, recording the bomb attack, perhaps indicating the name of the author, my move to London, possibly even my assumed name at this London hospital that does not wish to be identified.

Somehow I do not seem to mind so much the fact that as part of the price of imagining that my little bit of volition makes a difference to the historical process, I have been completely bureaucratized, desiccated and re-constituted into a multiplicity of files in many countries and many languages. It amuses the more philosophical side of me to think that today I do not even occupy space on paper, but have been reduced to a dot in a computer memory, that this wounded romantic, lone and palely waiting to receive his visitor, is in reality no more than a speck of current on a microchip.

If it is the friendly anti-terrorist man, I suppose he too has read up his files on me, perhaps even on my father, although Solly has been dead for many years. (Did they record the time he shouted at me for being a bloody unrealistic and romantic fool for not following his advice and becoming a barrister, in England I would soon be famous, and joining the Labour Party and becoming a Member of Parliament, and my answer, burning with hurt because my father was shouting at me, that it was he who had given me my values, he couldn't complain, and though I did not mention it, I wanted to say I still treasured the postcard discovered when I was leaving South Africa in which he wished me a happy sixth birthday, and may I grow up to be a soldier in the fight for liberation.) One of the pleasures of living in Mozambique was that I did not feel bizarre for holding the beliefs I did, since the country was full of soldiers in the fight for liberation, and anyone you met in the street or behind a counter could well have been a freedom-fighter. It was tiring during the years I lived in England having to hide what I regarded as the better, more altruistic side of my nature all the time, and maybe I am back to that now, with the sergeant representing in a most courteous form the scepticism that is so deep in this society and that I must learn to adjust to, since after all, and for all my criticisms of this country, England is the land that I have run to and that has received me after the two greatest crises in my life; and, more profoundly, perhaps this self-centred and passionless world (if you took away adultery there would be no passion at all) is the very normality we are fighting for so passionately in South Africa.

Is it my psychiatrist?

He first came to me the day after Margit told me the details of the explosion, and I have been grateful for his help ever since. I am not sure what I expected of him, I simply knew that I needed support from someone skilled in dealing with problems of the mind and the emotions. A buoyant person who listens well and talks well, he shares with me a certain common cultural background – he is the only person so far who already knew the joke about Himie Cohen – and, most important of all, he does not think I was mad to be staying in Mozambique at all. That is the one thing I could not have faced, the assumption that I was indulging some kind of death wish by being in the ANC and continuing to live in Maputo. Being in the ANC, well, that is just part of my life now, I cannot imagine any other, it is not just a question of belief, it has become part of my culture, it has affected every major action in my life, where I have lived, whom I have loved, what work I have done, the very conception I have of myself. As for staying in Maputo, that rejuvenated me; in England I picked up a vast amount of information, had vivid cultural and intellectual experiences, but did not learn one new thing, whereas Mozambique turned my head over several times and engaged my imagination and emotions all the way.

I do not expect the psychiatrist to agree with my views, or even to understand them, but I do need him at least to respect them. To take away my pride in myself would be the biggest disaster and make the loss of my arm quite meaningless. Maybe later in my life, I will look back on the decades of struggle and dreams and analyse objectively where I was right and where I was wrong. Right now I have no doubt that my struggle continues, the same struggle I have always been in, only this time in a different form, the struggle to get whole and active again, to triumph over the bomb attack. What sort of psychiatrist would it be who, in the name of helping me reconstruct my personality, took my élan and self-esteem away? In fact, there has been no problem. I think he is curious about me as a person, but sees his function as being to deal with me as a victim of trauma and nothing else. I imagine that if I were the one who had placed the bomb, and not the victim, he would ask the same questions and evaluate answers by the same criteria. He, like me, is obviously concerned to find the source of my brightness, and, unlike me, appears to be suspicious of it. I ask him what I should prepare myself for, and he tells me that the hard part comes after the physical recovery, when many patients find their morale suddenly collapsing. What happens to them? I ask. They become depressed and extremely irritable and find difficulty living with anyone. So I have been warned.

It seems that he is a specialist in disaster, dealing with victims of car accidents, industrial misfortunes, and more recently, survivors of a capsized ferry called the *Spirit of Free Enterprise*. Part of me is pleased with the notion of the democracy of disaster, that I am in essence no different from the mechanics and housewives and business people he has dealt with, part of me wishes to be unique, memorable, different from any other patient he has ever had. It appears that as his first bomb victim, I am extending his repertoire. Well, he is my first psychiatrist, so he is also extending mine.

Is it my surgeon?

He is the key figure in my treatment, and yet has physically done less for me than any of the nurses. I am lucky to have someone like him in charge of my case, I like the way he looks at you and talks to you; unlike some doctors, he knows that you have eyes that like to be looked at when you are addressed. He also speaks to you as though you have some intelligence and are at least mildly interested in what is happening to you, and, more rarely for a British doctor, does so even when in the presence of his colleagues. I cannot stand being discussed by doctors as if I were not there; perhaps it is an élitist thing in me, but I want to shout out: I am also a professional, and my brother is a doctor and I don't like this assumption that I am too ignorant to be included in the discussion. Another thing I like about him is that he speaks well of the treatment I received in Maputo, and does so without astonishment, in fact indicating that everything that could have been done was done.

His job has been to supervise my treatment and explain to me what is going on. Through him I have been referred to my internal medicine specialist, who gave my liver an especially thorough scan, cold jelly on my stomach and this machine running up and down up and down, checking whether it is okay after apparently having been ruptured by the blast and sewn together again in Maputo. (I am getting new details all the time; sometimes I wonder if I am not a little like a car that has been in an accident, you repair everything, but it is never quite the same again, there are always things just a little out of alignment.) He has also sent me to my radiographer, my eye specialist, my ear specialist, my orthopaedic surgeon, and now, with the problem of the drain, to two thoracic surgeons, the second of whom succeeded in really getting the lung clear. The only problem is that it has been discovered that I now have MRSA, that is, a multi-resistant bacterial infection, which means that visitors who come to see me have to put on gowns as part of what is called barrier treatment.

Is it my occupational therapist?

She is a quiet person and she teaches me tricks. She has promised to show me how to tie a shoelace with one hand, the only part of dressing that so far is beyond me. People ask if I am right-handed, er, sorry, was right-handed, and I reply that I was ambidextrous . . . equally useless with both hands. The fact is that my left hand is learning skills it never had before. D-O-G; the reporter from the *New York Times* was impressed by my writing page after page of D-O-Gs as he interviewed me. D, O and G belong to the same writing cluster, I have just learned, and so for practice I should write them together. Once, many years ago, it was the cat that sat on the mat. Today it is dog, and the interesting thing is that I am getting the same pleasure from dog as I once got from cat.

Most medical treatment is quite authoritarian. You cannot say today I feel like having my wounds cleaned, tomorrow I don't. But OT is very democratic and patient-centred. It is all up to you, what you want to do. Sometimes I wish she would at least make a few suggestions so that I could know what goodies they have to offer, and that I would not have to rack my brains to find intelligent answers when she asks me: well, what do you want OT for? I told her that I wanted to be able to dress myself, write, wash myself, cook for myself and play bridge. She jumped at the bridge idea, and some days later brought me a little stand for cards that she had had made in the workshop. My bridge-playing friends, who wish me a speedy recovery so that I can make up a fourth, tell me that they have improvised something far better for a bridge-playing comrade who had suffered a stroke, namely, a thick book with an elastic band placed around the spine, and I am happy to feed this information into OT Science. She also brought me a wooden backscrubber made in the workshop – I was obviously a good patient who put interesting demands on her department – and although I thanked her warmly, I did not say that I would rather the middle of my back remained unclean because the brush was ugly, and in my present state beauty came long before cleanliness. In fact, this was a problem, I had no friendly consultant on beauty, somehow it just did not fit into the medical programme. To whom could

I explain my almost violent desire to be surrounded by beautiful things, as if the serene blue and orange tones of a Matisse reproduction were as important to me as my bandages or leg exercises? When one friend asked me what I needed, the words came tumbling out, though I was embarrassed to be asking. I want a watch, I said, a beautiful watch that keeps good time, I've never had one, but it must be beautiful.

Is it my physiotherapist?

Something interesting is happening here, my body is in love with her as it is with the nurses, and she does not even touch me, just speaks. She gets me to breathe into a tube that has bouncing balls at the end, to stretch my short right arm (the exercise I like least, it is quite painful, and I hate the concentrated self-effort required; everything else is fun except these exercises), to lift my legs up and down, swing to the left, swing to the right, several times a day. She told me on the first day that she had dreaded coming to me after reading the case notes, I had seemed like a hopeless case with so many injuries, half blind, half deaf, how would she communicate with me? But in fact it was turning out to be easy. For my part I look forward to her visits, she brings out in me what in other contexts could be pure macho preening but which now is pride in the capacity of my body and muscles to function according to my will. I have two clear criteria for one day being better: running on the beach, preferably in Maputo, and dancing. I have to start preparing now, with umpteen boring lifts of my leg to get some tone back in my muscles (my poor legs, so thin and bony and weak and injured). As Samora said, victory does not just come, it has to be organized. Up to the left, up to the right, up to the left, up to the right.

Is it my limb-fitting engineer?

One of the few men in my life that actually touches me, he measured me like a tailor, and took a cast of my shoulder with cloth impregnated with plaster of paris that he soaked with water. He handles me with the ease of someone who spends his whole life dealing with amputees, and I feel comfortable with his hands on me, without any sense of bodily adoration, however. He examines what he calls my stump, pronouncing it stoomp, and informs me that it is just a bit too long for an elbow joint to be fixed on it, but that in due course I can have another operation to have it shortened, so that my arm and elbow come out at exactly the right size. Seeing that I am not enthusiastic about the idea, and being part of the non-authoritarian sector of treatment, he adds that it is all up to me, and that everything depends on what I want the arm for. Why does one want an arm? You want an arm so that you can have an arm, of course. Everyone wants an arm, in fact two, what a question. But when he asks me, I cannot say that I want an arm because I want my arm back, that sounds childish, and what will he think of me and of the ANC? So I say that I want an arm for functional reasons, for cosmetic purposes and for balance, one, two, three, like an exam question. What I want to say is that I would like to get my arm back for reasons of vanity, so that I can have the last laugh over the bombers, but I don't mention that, partly because I do not want to say anything at all, not even in the privacy of this hospital room, that might encourage the bombers to have another go.

Someone is turning the door handle, the door opens and I see with pleasure that the person who knocked and is now entering is my . . .

15

. . . physiotherapist.

'Now, stand.'

'What?'

'Stand up.'

'Are you crazy? I've got a broken heel, shattered to bits.'

'That's all right, you can stand on it.'

'I want to see it in writing, did the orthopaedic surgeon say I could?'

It is embarrassing for me to be arguing with the physiotherapist, though she seems rather to be enjoying my spirited words. When she asked me to manoeuvre myself to the side of the bed and then hang my legs over until they touched the ground, I thought this was a prelude to more exercises, boring but part of the way to organizing victory. But now she wants me to stand. My legs are far too feeble, she can see that; the muscles have almost gone, there is virtually no flesh there, and certainly no strength. It will hurt like anything, the pain will be mine, not hers. And the most important thing is that I might do permanent damage to the heel, the bones will break again and everything go out of shape, and I will have a misshapen heel for life.

'Okay, I'll get your notes.'

The problem is that the orthopod is in New Zealand, and there is no way of consulting him. While she is out of the room I find myself agonizing. I want to impress the physio, I want her to think I am the best patient she has ever had, I want her to have the highest regard for me (and for the ANC, even if she has never heard of it), but this idea of standing on a heavily fractured heel is just crazy. Please, I wish to say to her, my feelings are completely objective, and have absolutely nothing to do with the fact that you are a young female physiotherapist and not an older male consultant . . .

'Here we are, have a look.'

She has returned and shows me a page in rough scrawl in my file. I suspect she is violating some norm or another by letting me see the file, but now my doubts are beginning to have doubts, since she is so confident. I read through the description of my fracture and see the words: '. . . and should not bear pressure for six weeks.' Speaking as a lawyer, that is not exactly authorization for me to stand now, even though six weeks have passed.

'Okay, here goes.' I submit.

She is sitting in front of me, a table behind her, and above that a mirror on the wall. I let my legs down slowly, until I feel the unfamiliar sensation of carpet on my bare soles.

'Now sit forward as much as you can, tuck your bottom in and slowly stand.'

I lean forward, and nearly topple over and put my hand out to steady myself. Even this is not easy, my body weight seems strange, and I instinctively want to put out two arms simultaneously to keep upright. Inch by inch, pressing my toes lightly against the carpet, I wriggle from buttock to buttock to get nearer the edge of the bed. I look at her to see if I am in position. I have never thought about standing up before, I do not even remember what you do, I have always just stood up. She nods. I think of ways of postponing the moment of pressure. Who am I to tell my body that it must

68

stand, my leg that it must bear pain? It is as though there is a control tower in the top of my head – I am not sure if this control point actually has a location, or if I only think it must be in my head because I know my brain is there – sending out a message to the rest of me to prepare to rise.

'Can I use my hand to steady myself?'

'Yes, if you want. Go up slowly.'

I look down at my frail legs, at the Charlie Chaplin shorts. I do not want to topple over, maybe I will get further injuries, it will be so humiliating to fall. I cannot remember how you stand up, which are the muscles you have to tighten, what you do with your joints, how you move your body. I cannot do it, it is impossible, there must be a better way, she should hold my hand and help me up, the first time at least.

'Lean forward a little and keep your backside well tucked in.'

I lean slightly towards her, will my feet to press down on the carpet and urge my shoulders to rise. For a moment nothing happens, and then I feel empty space and lack of security under my backside. Slowly, slowly, I tell myself, don't rush, don't fall, she knows what she is doing, and if she says I can stand then I can surely stand. The floor seems a long way down, and I look to see if I would hit my head on anything if I were to tumble. Slowly, slowly. I am shaking a little and totally insecure, but I feel myself steadily rising. My backside is in the air, my knees still sharply bent, my body hunched forward, my hand pressing frantically on the mattress; never have I been so conscious of consciousness. I have done well so far, managed a lift-off, it is enough, I can topple back and try to stand tomorrow.

'Keep your bottom in.'

Well, this is it, the moment of risk, when I urge my toes and my knees and my bum and my waist and my shoulders and my head to loft themselves upwards into the open space above me, willing my corporeal mass to be upright and not to fall. There is an instant of panic as all the parts of my body come into motion; like the artist in the air between trapezes, I have committed myself to a movement I feel I cannot control and whose consequences I cannot determine. Head, backside, legs, shoulders, my arm, they seem like component parts of me receiving signals in an unco-ordinated way, there is no unison between my muscles and joints, no synthesis between different sectors of my body. Only my will and a sense that there is no going back seems to prevent me from disintegrating into my disparate parts, or just collapsing anarchically on to the floor under the force of gravity.

Something is happening over which I seem to have little command, it is just taking place through inertia. My knees are straightening, my backside is coming forward, and I feel more and more pressure on the balls of my feet and the palm of my hand. I look straight ahead, the first intimations of triumph beginning to enter my thoughts. In front of me is the physiotherapist, watching closely but not offering a hand. To keep myself steady, I look past her at the table and then to the wall.

There is the mirror, and slowly a strange sight comes before my eyes. I see some short-cropped hair entering the frame of the mirror, then a forehead and some staring eyes, solemn, expressionless, perhaps with just the slightest trace of amusement. The movement continues, and a complete long, thin face with cuts and scars on the right-hand side, is there.

70

Next, shoulders appear, bony and wrapped in bandages, and the outlines of a body standing up. This thin, scarred, bandaged, swaying image, with staring eyes and cropped hair, is me.

'Brilliant. Now sit down slowly, move your backside slowly and bend your knees . . .'

'Can I just try something? I'd like to try standing without using my hand.'

'By all means.'

I lift my hand from the bed and feel the heavy weight of my feet on the floor.

'Am I allowed to lean against the bed with my thighs?'

'Yes, if it helps you. But try without.'

I urge my body to lean forward and feel a gap opening between my thighs and the bed. For a few moments I am not in contact with the bed at all, I am upright and on my own and unsupported, I am standing, I am free, and I am triumphant.

Now, to get down again. When we climbed the mountain, getting down was always trickier than going up. I will my knees to bend slowly, my trunk to lean forward and my backside to begin jutting. Slowly, slowly, my fingers are on the mattress, but I am not pressing heavily on them, they are there just in case. I am going down, my trunk disappears from the mirror, then my shoulders, then my chin and nose and eyes, and finally my head altogether, so that all I can see is the table with a mirror above it and the physiotherapist. She is glowing.

'Wonderful, marvellous.'

I do not think I felt as proud when I was told that my PhD thesis had been accepted. Of one thing I am now sure, that when Jesus appealed to the lame and the halt to rise up and walk, he had a physiotherapist with him. And I have made a surprising discovery: whereas before my hair was beginning to go grey, it has now turned completely black with the shock.

16

'In a rare admission of defeat, Mr Robert Maxwell yesterday said he was abandoning his dream of building a world-wide engineering business alongside his publishing empire, and selling the industrial site of Hollis, the engineering and services company controlled by his Pergamon group.'

Six minutes and fourteen seconds. I count the words: 45. That is about eight words a minute, not very fast, but the occupational therapist said I would get faster. I put my head forward, held the pen as comfortably as I could in my left hand, straightened the paper, looked at the time, and said to my hand: write. My hand responded obediently and well, my whole body seemed to be straining and involved as I forced myself to form the letters as quickly as possible. I had no problem in imagining the shape of the words, but found myself whispering to my fingers . . . move up, now curve downwards, keep going, don't stop, a little loop upwards, break off and start a new word. There were moments when I imagined the pen of its own accord sliding all over the page, anarchically destroying my meaning; then words seemed to form themselves without conscious direction on my part, the hand just appeared to be writing automatically, later I was murmuring to myself letter by letter again, thinking through each stroke and movement. In the absence of a prosthesis, my left hand that formerly had just been there, ready to back up my right one when called upon, now had to do everything.

The passage came from the business section of *The Times*, usually one of the first pieces of newspaper to flutter down to the floor. I wonder if Mr Maxwell would have been pleased to know that the loss of his dream has fortuitously helped me reconstruct my writing. I am glad I do not have to choose between writing and walking, I am not sure which is more important to me. They tried to kill me because of my writing, and it is a sad reality that the bomb is mightier than the pen, even if bombs cannot be made without pens while pens can be made without bombs. But now I am writing again. It is not an intellectual activity, it is a sensual one, deeply physical, in which my whole body engages itself, and my mind at the same time. I am simply copying something as an exercise – what am I to Maxwell or Maxwell to me? – training my head and arm and fingers to move the pen along in accordance with my thoughts.

I agree with the critic who said that reading was not merely the mental absorption of a text, but a physical act in which the colour, weight and texture of the book, together with the physical context (beach, bed, comfortable chair, train) contributed towards the total experience. The occasion, the moment, enrich or impoverish the text, each book has a subjective meaning to the reader just as it once had to the writer. I remember almost nothing of the text of the 'biggest' book I have ever read, a huge volume of Proust which I found myself reading furiously, night after night, just before I was due to return to Africa, but I recall reading it not for itself but in order to understand references to it in my friend's thesis on femininity and the creative imagination, and that the book was difficult to balance on the blanket as I got through my quota of pages each night, while Stephanie, in the last period of our marriage, fighting against weariness after midnight, laboured over her political work in the room next door, and I also remember that I used a bright piece of silver paper to mark my slow but relentless progress through the pages of my most difficult read ever. Similarly, writing for me has always had an occasional or momentary character, so that I have memories of the act of writing, even the paper I used, but forget the letter or article or even book immediately after.

Soon I will be writing to my friends; this will be real writing in which my will shapes not only the letters but the thought itself. Yet the deep pleasure is not in composing the letter, not in the conjunction of words, but in imagining the emotion of the recipients at the special moment when they open the envelopes and discover who the writer was. If I can get a few jokes in, or a couple of vivid formulations, so much the better, but what matters, what really is being communicated, is that I have overcome the loss of my arm, and chosen to share this wonderful knowledge with them. In that sense, I cannot lose; the more shaky and spindly the handwriting, the more strongly the point is made.

I have whole plastic bags full of letters and cards that I have received over the weeks, far too many for me to answer in full. I will write to my mother in Cape Town, she will be coming to see me later in the year, and to friends in Maputo and Harare and New York. I will also take up the offer of my independent, vivacious, anarchic and super-intelligent friend to spend a holiday with her in her warm country; somehow as soon as I read her one-sentence invitation, I knew it was right. A small glow of pleasant anticipation starts up inside me, the first intimations of greater excitement to come when I actually start to write and begin to imagine the astonishment of the recipients as they find out whom the letter is from. Most of the correspondence will be sheer fun, and good exercise for my hand at the same time, much better than writing 'dog' a hundred times, or even copying the elegant *Times* prose. But there is just one letter that will be totally different; the subject is so painful to me that I do not even like to think about it.

There is a knock at the door, and I am pleased to see it is my comrade Wolfie, who is my postperson, my organizer of visits, my contact with the outside world, and my friend. Yesterday he brought me a letter that was different. Wolfie's support means a lot to me, certainly more than I will ever say, since I tend to go along with the idea that comradeship is just there, it does not declare itself. We say thank you to each other for passing the sugar or opening a door, but not for undertaking a hazardous mission or fulfilling a burdensome duty. After all, we are involved in a common endeavour to liberate our country, and the question of personal gratitude simply does not arise. What counts is the mutual willingness to contribute each according to our capacities – and yet, and yet, sometimes when I am the recipient of the specially delicate courtesy of our President Oliver Tambo, and when I recall the kindly graciousness of former President Chief Luthuli who made every member feel appreciated and valuable, I wonder whether perhaps there should not be more pleases and thank yous even amongst the most dedicated of freedom fighters. My comradeship with Wolfie goes back to when he was an ex-serviceman and I still a child, and I had placed a rugby ball on top of a door to fall on my brother's head (I was allowed to take the ball home after the game because I was so serious and dependable) and it fell on his head instead. He laughed, and he is still in the struggle. Another comrade to whom the same thing happened was very angry, and as he dropped out of the struggle not many years after I think it is a good test.

'Oh hell,' I say to Wolfie as he sits down by the side of my bed.

'What's the matter?'

'Did you know about the others?'

'What others?'

'The others who were hit when my car exploded?'

'Er . . . yes.' Wolfie does not like to say what he knows and what he does not know, he spent so many years doing clandestine work, including, he hints but never says outright even after twenty-five years, looking after Nelson Mandela in the underground.

The letter has taken me unawares, and I feel hints of depression beginning to attack me. I read several times the words that assail me, kindly words expressed with grace and tact: '. . . and we hope that you are satisfied with the arrangement whereby the bulk of the money collected goes to the family of Mr Mussagy who is still in a coma in the Central Hospital . . .'

So I was not the only victim, and my recovery is not a solo activity swept along by my personal elation. It appears from the letter that Mr Mussagy and his son had been walking along when they were hit by shrapnel from my car. The son was now out of hospital, while the father had first been sent to South

76

Africa for observation before being placed in the Central Hospital in Maputo. I know it has nothing to do with me, that the responsibility lies completely and utterly with those who placed the bomb, yet I cannot shake off a feeling of guilt, that the hatred directed at me hit the most innocent of passers-by.

Until now I have not thought much about those responsible for putting the bomb in my car, I have preferred to cocoon myself in the present and avoid re-inserting myself into the situation of confrontation and violence; let Security worry about catching those who did the deed, that is not my problem, my problem is to get better.

One of the strongest and most vivacious letters I received, from a very dear comrade who had spent twelve years on Robben Island, told me not to worry, the attack on me would be fully avenged. The directness of the letter moved me, but not the thought of vengeance. Perhaps there is something wrong with me, but the idea of an eye for an eye, a tooth for a tooth, an arm for an arm, fills me with anguish. Is that what we are fighting for, a South Africa filled with armless and partly blind people? Is that what freedom means? There is only one kind of vengeance that can assuage the loss of my arm, and that is a historical one: victory for what we have been fighting for, the triumph of our ideals.

Yet all these thoughts were easy when I was the only victim, when it seemed to be a personal question for me to work out in my own mind alone. Now the explosion has a different and more tragic dimension: a piece of my car is lodged in the head of a Mozambican who was taking his son for a walk, this is attempted murder. (I have a half-memory of exam questions that I used to set as a law lecturer, and how frequently did we joke with the intrinsic insensitivity of criminal law teachers about life imitating exam questions: A kills B intending to kill C . . .) For the first time I feel stirrings of anger, not on my own behalf, but on behalf of the others hit by the shrapnel. I cannot help wondering if part of my anger is not based on a sense of disappointment at having my elation punctured, at having lost my monopoly status as victim with sole right to determine levels of rage. I wish I could talk to Wolfie about these things, but it all seems so super-subjective, so personal and introspective, that I hold back. I have asked Wolfie to discourage visitors from talking about the bomb. In any event, I do not know what the problem really is, how to articulate these strange and uncomfortable feelings I have, and I could not bear the simple answer that it is nonsense to take on to myself the burden of Mr Mussagy's injuries, that I have to look at the question politically and not personally, etc., etc., exactly the sort of reply I myself would give to someone in my position.

Wolfie has once and possibly twice in his life been a soldier, first in the war 'up north' as we used to say, against Hitler, then perhaps he was associated with the early armed combatant units of the ANC in 1961. Perhaps soldiers look at these things differently, perhaps it is easier, more impersonal for them. The ethical questions are converted into issues of courage and discipline connected with joining or not joining in armed struggle, relationships with superiors or subordinates in the command structure, methods of struggle that might or might not be used. They do not involve questions of relationship with victims. Perhaps there are no victims, only enemies, so that the only point in issue is the definition of who are enemies. But I am not a soldier and have difficulty de-personalizing these questions.

Once when I was younger I dreamed of becoming a guerrilla, and wondered if I would have the courage to live the life of a freedom fighter up in the hills. Then I abandoned the idea for an entirely non-political reason. I must have torn something in my knee-caps when I ran recklessly down Table Mountain, week after week, faster and faster, and after a day of walking my knees would simply give in. In any event, when the ANC was driven underground in 1960, I was asked to carry on with my legal and public activity, which I did, until I was banned and arrested.

I decided not to ask Wolfie his opinion on these questions. I am not ready for a balanced discussion, all I can think of is bombs, their bombs, our bombs, so many bombs, the best of our side and the worst of theirs assembling bombs, doing their recces, putting the bombs where they are to explode, and then trying to vanish. Perhaps the greatest of the many crimes of apartheid has been the way it has forced the finest people of our generation, the most courageous and selfless, the most idealistic and romantic, the most intelligent and capable, to devote their energies and skills to the art of war. Their debates and theorizing are about the difference between armed propaganda and people's war and arming the masses, and whether we have been in an insurrectionary or pre-insurrectionary situation. My preoccupations with myself and this half-sense of guilt I feel as I lie on this hospital bed do not seem very relevant. This is the strange situation I am in, there are thousands of our people living in hard conditions in camps, surviving in the underground, struggling in detention and in prison, who have chosen options I never did, who have accepted far greater risks than I ever have, who have fought harder and more tenaciously than I, and been braver by far, yet I, who followed an easier road, and who had the chance of having a family, and pursuing a profession and writing and travelling, am called a hero, because of the fortuitous reason of having survived a bomb blast while their individual deeds are virtually unknown. The part that is really strange is not the injustice of my over-recognition and their under-recognition, but the pride and joy these comrades take in my survival. I become a symbol to them of courage and indestructibility when really I am not particularly brave at all, just someone with a certain talent for dealing with some of the intimate problems of the movement, a tendency for introspection, a dash of humour and a vast admiration for their real courage.

Wolfie can see that I have things on my mind, but is too tactful to press me. He mutters something about being rather busy – ANC comrades are always rather busy, it is part of our way of life, we fill our lives with meetings and appointments and activities of every kind – and leaves me to my reflections.

I pick up my pen, place the pad and board on my lap, and begin writing furiously.

'In a rare admission of defeat, Mr Robert Maxwell yesterday said he was abandoning his dream of a world-wide building [engineering] business alongside his publishing one [empire], and selling the industrial site of Hollis, the engineering and service company controlled by his Pergamon group.'

I look at the time, 6 minutes and 30 seconds, that is, 16 seconds longer than the previous time, and two mistakes.

17

The corridor seems endless as I shuffle along, my stick going forward first, then my right foot parallel, then my left foot through. I must remember to keep the triangle as the physio showed me, never the stick and the two feet in a straight line, but always foot through or stick through. Who would have imagined that walking just a few yards could require so much thought and concentration? Apart from the pain in my foot, the worst is the fear that someone walking from behind will bump into me and knock me over. I must try to get a natural rhythm, must try to think of something else and let my legs think for themselves.

The offer I have just received to go to Columbia University in New York for a few months early next year sounds good. The physio said it would be nine months before I could run, and two years before I felt normal again and moved unconsciously and instinctively. I am sure I can reach these goals more rapidly. I did not ask her about when I can travel, when I can study and when I can teach. I like the USA, always have, ever since my first visit there in 1974, after I had agonized for weeks about whether I should accept Ford Foundation funds to attend a conference. No one could agonize like me in those days. I remember once standing in a queue at the university self-service restaurant in Maputo and holding everybody up because I had to take an orange from a tray on the counter, and the problem was that the orange near me was a bit shrivelled, and I was not sure if a good revolutionary took the orange that was nearest or the orange that was best.

A few more steps, and I can rest on the chair near the stairs. The physio is very practical; she knows that as soon as my infection is cleared, I will be going to my brother's flat, which is on the second floor. So I go to the stairs at the end of the corridor and practise climbing steps.

I took the nearby, shrivelled orange. Years later I agonized again in the USA. I was on a speaker's tour, and my friends were all offering me pot. Even the guy who met me at Logan Airport offered me some as I emerged from the baggage reclaim, and all across the States, even at Madison where the mayor's wife offered brownies enriched with marijuana. I had never smoked it, the police used to try to trap us with it in South Africa, and I was pretty puritan on the subject. I always said in a very prim voice, no thank you, until I reached LA and Santa Monica on the West Coast, and it was Easter weekend and I had no speaking engagements, and I had just met Jane Fonda dressed up as a rabbit giving eggs to her children, and seen people jogging backwards on the beach, and the person offering me was a great feminist radical (not radical feminist) lawyer whom I loved and trusted very much, and I said yes.

At last, I have reached the chair and I can rest my exhausted body and ease my aching foot. Whenever I put on the walking boots that my brother has brought me, I do not know if I will suffer from the fierce pain that from time to time shoots across the sole of my right foot and makes walking an agony. Tying the laces has turned out to be easy; if even I can do it with my inept fingers, it must be so. The trick is to catch one end of the lace with a knot at the bottom end of the shoe and then do a single lace-up so that what emerges at the top is only one end of the lace rather than two – it is then not too difficult to tie a single bow with one hand, over the top, make a loop and pull the loop through.

I also ran on Santa Monica beach, though only forwards, and whenever I am in New York I make a point of running round the reservoir in Central Park, always twice. On only one visit to New York did I fail to do this jogging circuit, and that was when I was ill with mononucleosis in that terrible year after Ruth was killed. Instead I went on what seemed an unending walk to find the 57th precinct or 78th, I do not recall the number now, in search of protection against bombs. I had been referred there by the Police Commissioner for Human Rights, which was the nearest my civil rights lawyer friends had been able to get me to someone who knew about assassinations and how to avoid them. I was so amazed at the way the precinct seemed to have been copied from a *Kojak* set, with people dashing around all the time and shouting at each other with little regard for rank, that I even forgot I had mono. Come to think of it, the sergeant from the anti-terrorist unit was as different from my friendly policeman from Scotland Yard as New York is from London – perhaps the police are the highest or at least most quintessential form of cultural expression of any country. If I was nervous before I spoke to him, I was terrified afterwards. He told me of more ways of being killed than I had thought possible, including having a hole cut in the ceiling to let the assassin through, and suggested I go to work wearing a bullet-proof vest. I decided that buying an alarm for my car was a more realistic proposition, and smiled to myself at the irony of the fact that he, an African American policeperson in New

York, could never quite work out that this respectable white South African lawyer, who must be a good guy because he had been referred by the Commissioner, actually belonged to what he would have regarded as a subversive organization and feared assassination by terrorists sent by the South African Government, whom he would have regarded as a legitimate authority.

It is time to get up and launch myself on the stairs. I should climb them at least once a day, but I seem to look for any excuse to get out of the painful tramp along the corridor. Remember the formula for standing up – sit forward, tuck my bottom in and rise slowly. Good. It is just a few yards to the stairs.

What snobbery I have goes to the US rather than England. I do not think I could ever be seduced by upper-class England, but I could in the US if they mixed in enough architecture and music and modern art and the *New York Times* and the *New Yorker* and ice-cream. I feel completely at ease at Columbia or Harvard and get a headache every time I go to Oxford or Cambridge, even though I have very good friends there. I justify everything I enjoy in the States on the basis that it is racist South Africa and its supporters in the US who want to keep us away from Americans, who wish to isolate us in ideological laagers, while we are trying to pierce the boycott being imposed on us. We are not terrorists, we are ordinary, decent people fighting for simple justice in our country, and we have every right to associate with all strata of American society, not just our natural allies amongst the oppressed communities. I cannot say it is actually my revolutionary duty to go to the Met or the City Opera in New York, but it is certainly not against our struggle to go there nor to be friendly with people who love going there. And yet I wonder why I have

84

always to convince myself that it is all right politically. So many things are happening at the same time: clothes, beauty, Scotland Yard, Columbia University, and, yes, Ford Foundation. One of the first persons to send me a get-well telex was the East Africa representative of the Ford Foundation, and I was delighted. He went on to ask if I needed help in any way to carry on with the kind of projects I had been doing in Mozambique with their funds, and I dictated to my brother a proposal to complete a book that Gita and I were preparing on the evolution of the Mozambican legal system. (If I cannot work out a project proposal, I know I am dead.)

Good foot up to heaven, bad foot down to hell. You would think it was the easiest thing in the world to remember how to climb and descend stairs, but each time I have to work it out: relatively speaking, my left foot is my good one, so I must lead with it when I start climbing. Then I must lift my stick and hold it in the air as I grasp the rail with my left hand. Now what do I do? Oh yes, I press down with my left foot and pull with my hand until I have swung my right foot up to the level where my left foot is.

Every step costs so much effort, so much concentration, and always the terror that someone is going to come running by and send me crashing. Slowly, steadily, I climb the stairs, foot, stick and hand, other foot. I wish I could rest, have something to drink, there must be a less exhausting way of getting better. Yet of all my exercises I like climbing the stairs the most, it reminds me somehow of the effort in climbing Table Mountain all those years ago, the tiredness in the thighs and the pressure on the lungs. At last I am at the top . . .

And then there is that other America, the one that

quietly caught me by surprise, the visit to Fiske College in Tennessee, that made me feel I was out of exile and back in Cape Town, and brought back to me how the American Paul Robeson had made us in Africa feel proud of our African-ness . . . Now for the descent. The stick is a nuisance on the stairs, yet I cannot discard it. Bad foot down to hell, my right foot descends tentatively. The important thing is to concentrate hard, think about each move and go slowly. My left leg is beginning to regain some shape since I have made it into my 'good foot', while my right leg is still skeletal. One step, two steps, three steps . . . The physio is very pleased with my progress, she says I am doing really well . . . I think I will go to the USA, yes, yes, yes . . . Eleven steps, twelve steps, I am down. Now it is back along the corridor, pushing open the door, and letting myself back into the room and the comfort of my bed. I must say that the newspapers strewn all over the floor look pretty disgusting.

18

I am keyed up, excited, jubilant; the thought of soon sliding into my first bath and covering my poor wounded body with water, fills me with total, uncomplicated happiness. I have always loved bathing, that first delicious moment as you plunge into the water and feel its cosseting heat on your skin, then the pleasure of total immersion as the water swallows and caresses you, and finally the long, dream-filled soak when your imagination takes over and all sorts of problems solve themselves by themselves. For those of us fortunate enough to grow up with bathrooms, the world is divided into shower-people and bath-people; showers are for cleanliness and freshening up, baths are to make you feel good, and I am definitely a bath-person.

I put the towel down, and start the complicated process of disrobing, as I look around the bathroom. There is something wrong with it, I am not sure exactly what – it has a bath, and taps and a bathmat, now a towel, and yet seems to be deficient somehow. There is no intimacy here, no sign of personal habitation, no damp facecloths and half-used tubes of toothpaste, none of the secret confusion of powders and pills and conditioners that each one of us has in a real bathroom; this is just a space with bathing facilities. Never mind, the nurse who is accompanying me has turned on the taps and soon I will be plunging into the lovely warm water and imagining intimate surroundings.

I pull the track-suit top over my head and with my left hand until it is all off save for the left sleeve, and then grip the edge of the sleeve in my teeth and manoeuvre that part off as well. I do not think anyone told me about using my teeth as a substitute hand, it seemed to come naturally; I surprise myself sometimes by the gusto with which I tackle the problems of daily living.

The familiar sound of rushing water intoxicates me further, setting up expectations of imminent skin pleasure. The nurse is beckoning me to ease my nude body on to a platform she has placed across the bath. I had not realized that getting in and out of the bath was going to present difficulties, I thought you just got in. The plank is cold on my backside, and jars against the mood of anticipated enjoyment I have been trying to maintain. I feel precarious and uneasy as I sit on it and slowly hoist my thin legs over the side and into the bath. My feet penetrate the water, pleasurably shocked by its liquidity and heat, but I am unsteady and ask the nurse for support. She holds my arm and advises me to let myself down slowly on to a plastic seat she has placed in the bath so that I can then descend gently into the bath itself. This is getting increasingly complicated, more like one of those exercises I hate than a fun thing like having a bath.

The movement from the platform to the seat is ungainly, and there is an instant of panic as I leave the platform and feel myself unsupported and out of control. Normally when you want to do something, you just think to yourself, okay, now I will get up or go down or open the window, or whatever, and once you have decided you find your body just doing these things automatically. Now it is all different: I know clearly what I want to do, but I no longer know how to do it. I have consciously to will my different muscles to function, to speak to the various parts of my body. The greatest problem is directing messages simultaneously to different sectors, telling my arm to do one thing, my right leg to do something else, the muscles on my left side to do a third thing and then co-ordinating all the movements.

With an uncomfortable bump I topple rather than ease myself on to the plastic stool, encouraged by the fact that within moments I will at last be feeling the water creeping sensuously over my skin. For weeks I have been imagining my first happy plunge into the water, the moment of turn-around when my body ceases to be the recipient of injury and starts once more to become the vehicle of pleasure. I am on the brink of that momentous instant and hold back slightly so that I can enjoy it with total physical consciousness. Now.

Placing my left hand on the side of the bath, I take a breath and slide into the water. Adrenalin shoots into me, something is wrong, I am toppling over to my right, I am going to go under and swallow water, nurse, nurse, please help me. My left arm shoots out instinctively to correct my balance, but I have no right arm to steady myself with, and find myself rolling over even more heavily. I am half submerged, my whole body feels lop-sided and displaced, and the water splashes threateningly around me. This is disastrous, I want to leap out of the bath but cannot. Relaxing myself with a major effort of will, I succeed in gripping the side of the bath and slowly pull myself upright, trembling with exertion and fear.

Nurse, nurse, I want to say, hold my hand, comfort me, tell me everything will be all right, that I am a lovely person, help me, help me. I want to cry, to weep long tears, but I need someone to hold my hand. I have been betrayed by the water, my body feels treacherous, I was a fool to imagine happiness, nurse, help me, help me.

I am sure she will respond if I ask her out loud, but I feel deeply inhibited. She might misunderstand, we are alone here, I am nude and she is clothed and her job is to help me in and out of the bath and to wash my back, not to partake in gestures of physical affection. If I were dressed, I think I could cry in her presence and even ask for physical comfort, but not when I am naked. I say nothing, just feel desperate.

I sit disconsolately for a short while, and then reach for the soap. At least I can clean myself well. Keeping myself upright requires active concentration; presumably the one arm normally keeps the body steady while the other soaps. It was easier washing myself while seated in a chair next to the basin, I did not have this disconcerting feeling of bodily displacement in the water. I hate the bath, I hate being here, I hate the water, I hate my optimism, my imagination. The reality is that I have been severely mutilated and my body has lost its equilibrium. All the confidence I gained when walking turns to nothing when I enter the element of water.

The nurse appears to have no inkling of my severe agitation. I decide to ask her to soap my back so that at least I have some physical contact, but what I really want to do is to weep and weep and throw my body down and lament unrestrainedly. I am trapped in the bath and have to go through several labours before I can be alone with myself in my room. Every action intensifies my feeling of emotional rupture, the nurse's cheerfulness seems out of place and I resent her professional hand on my back. I ask her to wash the soap off, and in a low voice tell her that I think I have had enough of bathing for the first time.

Getting out of the bath is even more difficult than getting in. My muscles seem incapable of doing what I want of them, I just seem to have no force in my body. Always I have the fear of toppling and being unable to get my balance back. The worst is the moment of transition from one posture to another, when my backside has lifted itself from the bottom of the bath but not yet made contact with the surface of the stool. The panic comes from the feeling of lack of control, of physical self-consciousness and clumsiness. Now, in the depths of my misery, is the time when I need all my resolution and courage. This is not a fun venture on to the commode, where I fight only against stiffness and inertia, enjoying the joke of affirming my existence by the act of shitting, this is a battle to keep command of myself in the midst of intense emotional pain, a difficult defensive struggle to give me time to recover my sense of enjoyment and optimism.

With the help of the nurse I struggle on to the platform across the back of the bath, and then lift my legs over and on to the floor. There is no soft mat to receive my feet, nothing to hold on to when I laboriously turn my body round and begin to rise. I am short of breath and feel irritated by the cold sensation of the floor. In order to dry myself I have to sit down on a stool, which soon is covered with water draining off my body. There are parts of my body that I cannot reach with the towel, yet at this moment I do not want the nurse to touch me. Eventually I put my fruit salad shorts on over still damp thighs, and struggle to pull the track-suit top over my head and shoulders. Silent and stricken, I put on my boots, lace them up and begin the slow walk back to my room.

My few worldly goods are in plastic bags neatly standing in a row awaiting my departure. My farewell notes, each one different and carefully written with my left hand, each with a flower and roller-ball pen attached, are placed side by side on a tray, ready to be given to the nurses and to Eddie after I have gone. Nearly three months have passed since the explosion, and the first phase of my recovery is nearing its end. My friendly policeman has given me a little booklet to read on security; my psychiatrist has discussed the problems of transition with me, and incidentally made observations about love that interested me, one being that my relationship with Lucia was over even if she was going to come to London to see me during her next holidays, pity being a poor basis for love, another that patients usually fell in love with someone who was helping them; my surgeon has said that my remaining wounds have been healing well, congratulated me on the speed of my recovery and arranged for me to have a letter for my general practitioner; my occupational therapist has shown me how to tie a necktie (the trick is to secure one end to your shirt with a clothes-peg), given me a letter for the OT department at my nearest hospital, and taken back the clipboard on which I learned to write; my physiotherapist, one of the four of my helpers with whom I have fallen in love, has told me that now that I have mastered the basics of walking, climbing stairs and keeping my balance, my progress will be rapid. When she asked if I had any queries, I said yes, how soon could I make love again? and she replied that sexual intercourse was very tiring and it could still be a long way off. She has also given me a letter for the gymnasium of the nearby hospital, and reclaimed the breathing apparatus with plastic balls.

Knock, knock. This time I know who is coming, it is my friendly comrade. He is in England to prepare his participation in a walk from Glasgow to London to mark Nelson Mandela's 70th birthday. A former Robben Islander himself, we wrote a book together in Maputo on his prison experiences which was published in Britain and the USA and translated into many languages. For years we were on the same committees in Maputo, we played bridge together and whenever I went away on holiday I lent him my car. We were like brothers, and fought with the intimacy and intensity of brothers. Ironically, he had always been regarded as one of the targets for a bomb or a commando raid, not me. It happened that in the week of the explosion he was in Maputo, and I had promised to drive him to the airport. The day after the bomb, he was one of the first visitors to manage to see me, and he had come in with such a grim face that I had told him to smile, I was fine; I had also apologized for not being able to drive him to the airport.

The door opens, and he walks in. He has a huge smile on his face, and when he begins to talk to me, he keeps up the grin and forces the words through it.

'Well, my dear friend,' he says through his smiling teeth, 'and how are you feeling today?'

'You want to know how I'm feeling?' I ask in reply, aware of a terrible sense of aggression welling up within me.

'You want to know how I'm feeling?' I repeat.

My friend and comrade has put up with brutal interrogators and stern prison camp commanders, he has fought robustly with his friends as well as his enemies, and is not going to be put off by a note of irritation in my voice.

'Yes,' he says, still grinning. 'That's why I've come to see you.'

'How do you think I feel?' The words come rushing out, I have no control. 'I feel like shit, what do you think? How would you feel if you were blown up by a bomb and thrown yards into the air and came crashing down and fractured all sorts of bones and had your arm cut off and lost the sight of your eye, how would you feel? how would you feel? how do you expect me to feel? I feel like shit, that's how I feel. I feel like shit.'

The smile remains on his face, but only by an act of will on his part. I regret every word I say, but cannot stop myself. One day I will make up to him for this outburst, I will not tell him about the bath, he would not see the relevance, nor will I say that I am scared about what will happen when I leave hospital, because he stood up to any amount of torture and does not acknowledge that fear exists, I will simply be warm and friendly as we always are and the episode will lose itself in the wider story of enduring comradeship. Right now I only wish he would shout back at me, really loudly, so that I can shout at him some more.

THREE

19

The ball goes up into the air, the arm and racquet
come crashing down, thigh muscles taut, whole body
swinging forward, a desperate look on the champion's
face as he serves for an 'important point'. This is the
first time in ten years that I am watching Wimbledon
on TV, and far from getting the unalloyed pleasure I
expected, I find myself fascinated and slightly repelled
by the close-up muscularity. It is not the running around
the court that unsettles me, nor the overhead smashes
or volleys, it is the strain on the faces and in the bodies
of the players as they serve, their nervousness and the
sense that they are doing all this just for money. I have
been outside the world of competition for so long that
I find myself shocked by the brutal confrontation of
will against will. It was not that we lacked challenge
in Mozambique, on the contrary the nation's life was
at stake, we confronted everything, powerful neighbours, centuries of superstition, every form of racial
and cultural complex, cyclones, floods and hailstorms,
but never with this ferocious individual aggression and
combativeness. Similarly, in the hospital I always felt I
belonged to the caring part of Britain, I paid for some
items, not for others, but never had the sense that I
was obliged to compete with money for the right to
be treated.

After living for so long in an environment where
the will has been directed towards saving and helping
others, it is disconcerting to discover once more that
vast universe out there where volition is concentrated

solely on destroying the wills of others. Although the commentators speak about the grace and beauty of the shots, that is not what we are really watching; the skill and elegance are subordinated to the gladiatorial aspect, the essence of the spectacle is the encounter, where the success of the one is the defeat of the other. What is happening to me? I wonder; I'm becoming as squeamish about tennis as I am about boxing.

Prr . . . prr . . . prr . . . The phone is ringing, or rather it is making that piping-purring sound that phones make here these days, they have stopped actually ringing. I lean forward, reach for my stick, and heave myself up. Prr . . . prr . . . I count automatically, on the assumption that callers will wait for ten rings before hanging up. Once there used to be 'the phone', it was always in the same place, it looked like a phone and was easy to find. Now there is an apparatus in each room, and they do not look like telephones anymore, and some are portable and even cordless, and with so many in the flat of my brother and his companion, I can never locate any one of them. Prr . . . prr . . . seven. A severe spasm of pain shoots across the sole of my right foot, but I cannot stop moving, otherwise the caller will ring off. At last, I have found the phone, it is the white cordless one cradled against the white wall. I plunge in an ungainly way down on to the chair nearby, and pick up the receiver. I can never remember which way to hold it up, and whether I switch the battery on before or after use. Prr . . . prr . . . eight, nine.

'Hullo,' I shout desperately at the plastic oblong in my hand. I can hear a voice at the other end, but the TV commentator's voice is too loud, and there are bursts of applause. 'Hold on a moment,' I plead. I move to the edge of the chair, pull myself upright,

grab the stick and hobble over to the TV set to turn down the volume – the remote control belongs to the set in the bedroom. Each time I put pressure on my right foot, I feel intense pain, if there were someone present I would talk about agony, but there is only me and the person at the other end of the phone.

'Hullo,' I say once again, 'Sorry to keep you waiting.'

'Is that Dr John Sachs?'

'No, it's his brother, Johnny is at work, can I take a message?' As I am saying this, I hear my stick falling over on to the carpet. Damn.

'Can you ask him to phone me when he gets in this evening, my number is . . .'

'Just hold the line a minute while I get a pen.' I shuffle my backside along the chair to get nearer the stick, but it is just beyond my reach. I lean forward as far as I can, but if I stretch out too much with my left arm there is no way I can support myself. Damn. I will have to manage without it. I lever myself up, and start to look for paper. There are some discarded envelopes in the waste paper basket; if I walk carefully around the chair holding on to its back, and then lower my trunk carefully, I can just retrieve one. The sharp pain in my right foot is intolerable but I have to tolerate it. Now, where can I find a pen? There was one in this room, but I must have put it in the other room when I was writing a letter last night. I hobble back to the phone.

'Sorry to keep you, but I have to go to the other room.'

This time I will have to find a way of picking up the stick. Let's see, if I sit in the other chair and use my left foot, maybe I can roll it towards me. Gingerly I hook my heel over the end of the stick and manoeuvre it slightly towards me. Then, leaning forward carefully, and feeling my armpits moistening with sweat from the exertion, I grab the end of the stick and lift it up.

The stabs of pain in my foot are excruciating. I try pressing on the side of the foot, on the heel, on the other side, nothing seems to help. The journey of a few yards to the other room seems endless and filled with an enormous amount of furniture and doors that I have to negotiate. The room is dark, I have to be careful not to fall over as I lift my hand with the stick in it to switch on the light. I look everywhere for the pen, there are papers everywhere, and books, and my brother's computer and all sorts of documents, but no pen. I thrash through the papers, push the documents aside, look at the back of the computer, but no pen. I look around for the phone in this room, and with a sense of relief discover I am standing right next to it.

The problem of which end of the receiver to speak into is the same. I experiment with both sides and finally manage to get through.

'I'm very sorry to have kept you so long,' my apologies get lengthier with the delay, 'but I don't seem to be able to find a pen. Can I give you my brother's number at work?'

The caller agrees, and I ask him to wait while I look for the telephone directory. The journey back to the lounge is slow and painful, but at least I manage to find the directory immediately. Damn, damn, damn, I am not sure what Johnny keeps his number under, is it under J or under S or under H for Hospital or under I for Immunology, or is it under the name of the London hospital that does not wish to be identified? Ah, I have got it . . . but I cannot read it because my glasses are in the other room. If I use the stick, which I have to

100

do, I cannot carry the directory to the other room, that's the problem of having literally to do everything single-handed, so I will have to hobble next door to fetch my glasses and hobble back again.

The flickering images on the TV screen distract me as I lumber past, stick forward, leg parallel, leg through, stick forward . . . The pain and sense of exhaustion continue, I feel like throwing myself on to the couch and forgetting the caller and forgetting the tennis and forgetting everything except that life is impossible and that I am suffering not so much from bomb blast as from culture shock, but I push myself on, and after a little search, manage to locate my glasses and then holding the case in my teeth, to shuffle back to the lounge once more.

'I really am terribly sorry to have kept you waiting all this time, but my brother's number is . . .'

The phone call is over. Years ago in Cape Town our youth organization put on cultural festivals at which African groups from the townships performed comic sketches, and the one that always got enormous roars of laughter from the African comrades was that of the peasant recently arrived from the countryside employed by whites who tell him to look after the house and answer the phone while they are out . . . the phone rings and he does not know what to do. I do not want to see those damned athletes on the box, I cannot stand the excited murmurs of the commentators, the applause of the crowds. I just want to curl up and cry, and I cannot even curl up properly because my right side is still full of wounds. Today I am that peasant.

I hobble over to the TV set and turn up the volume again. The programme has changed, it is still sport, but this time it is athletics, and the run-up to the Olympic

Games in Seoul. They are showing women javelin throwers at a recent competition, 'Britain's brightest hopes for gold'. Somehow I do not seem to mind this kind of competition, it is each trying to do better than the other, but not to destroy the other. The physical effort, the moment of lunge, captivate me, and I find myself saying sadly to myself that now I will never hurl a javelin again, even though I have never thrown one in my life. I say the same thing when I see serves in tennis, or long drives in golf, even though I have not played tennis for twenty-five years and golf for twenty. It is like the joke about the mother complaining that her injured son will never play the violin again like Jascha Heifitz, only I cannot remember the joke.

Pawk . . . pawk . . . pawk . . . pawk . . . I can't believe it. There is a raucous sound coming from the other room, and that can only mean one thing, I forgot to replace the receiver there. So back I go, my stick and my hobble and my pain, and my sense of confusion and being overwhelmed. I know things will get better, that I will become physically stronger and able to walk more freely, that I will overcome my post-hospital helplessness and begin to organize my life so that I have pencil and paper near the phone and remember to carry my glasses with me, but right now I feel awful and only wish that those who think I am a hero could see me now as I really am. This is the real hard struggle; the words of Samora beat against my mind – victory comes from a myriad of trivial daily actions – but they bring me no comfort this time.

Pew . . . pew . . . pew . . . It is the intercom from the front door, I cannot stand it, I have to endure the painful walking once again.

'Who is it?' I ask wearily.

'It's me, Melba.' It is a woman's voice, rapid and with a strong Spanish accent.

'Oh, Melba, wonderful . . . come . . . come . . . come up.'

20

First my trousers slide down to the carpet. She offers to help me, but I refuse. Then I struggle to pull my top over my head, and this time, without asking, she takes hold of the garment and peels it off me. I am completely naked, shivering a little, and aware of how frail and stick-like my legs are. Now, at last, nude, wounded and pietà-like next to her elegantly clad body . . . the blissful moments I have been waiting for.

Melba. Long curly and wavy black hair, dark, dark eyelashes, and large smiling white teeth, she came flying into the flat, her coat coming off to reveal the sombre but highly chic clothing she always wears, and talking and looking for the Hoover and collecting up the laundry and putting something down in the kitchen and wasting not a moment and smiling at me, a large, expressive mouth, faint freckles on the rim of her face, dark mauves and browns and black in her dress, and I felt better right away, although I was not going to give up my sadness without a bit of a struggle.

'Are you good today?' she asked me.

' "How are you feeling today?" ' I corrected her. She is in London to study English.

'You feeling how today?' she tried again.

' "How are you feeling today?" '

'How you feeling today?'

103

'Terrible, thank you.'

'No, you have not to . . . er . . . must not feel like so.'

'But I do. I just want to lie down and cry.'

'No,' she was shocked, upset. 'The men not cry.' She was stuffing clothing into the washing machine, putting powder in the trays, looking around for the Hoover, so much energy.

'Maybe in Colombia they don't, but here I do; we should do it more often.'

'What the problem?' The machine was on, rumbling loudly and I could not hear her very well.

'Everything. I just feel like it. My prosthesis, I'm having trouble with it. I've got a boil on my ankle and it hurts every time I touch it, and sometimes I just feel sad, we have a right to feel sad, why is everyone telling us to be happy all the time?'

'No, you have not to cry, the men not cry.' Non-stop activity, by now she was hoovering and its roar added to the agitated rumble of the washing-machine. 'I make you *comida*, food, you feel better. I bring special food.'

'Can you make the omelette with sweetcorn, maize?'

'You like?' Her face was aglow. Conversation with Melba is not just an exchange of words, it is an encounter in which her personality projects openly, full of smiles, frowns and chuckles as she whizzes round the flat, her emotion at the surface, ready to be delighted and injured in an instant, not like our English talking where the words are everything and the feeling is saved up or rather buried down for special occasions.

'I love it, I love it. You make the omelette while I lie down and have a little cry.'

I shuffled along to my bed, let myself down carefully,

rested my forehead in the elbow of my left arm, and began to sob softly. I do not like crying in an empty flat, nor when someone is right with me; when I am feeling weepy like this is almost the only moment when I do not want to be stroked and comforted, it is a deeply intimate thing between me and myself, yet I like to have someone within calling distance who knows that I am sad. I wished I could cry more powerfully, and that really profound emotion would come out, but it was gentle crying as usual, a few little spasms and a couple of tears. I rocked my head slowly, felt the comfort of the pillow on my face, and let the quiet shuddering travel along my body.

Melba was standing at the door, distraught at seeing me in distress, on the verge of real and deep tears herself. 'Come to *la cosina*, the kitchen,' she urged me, suddenly brightening. 'Is big surprise.'

I got up, took my stick and stumbled along to the kitchen. I was not feeling so bad really, I just need these periodical little weeps to purge myself of trapped emotion. There are different levels of happiness and unhappiness that have little to do with each other – I often felt that I was happy in Mozambique even when I was unhappy, and fear that I will be unhappy in England even when I am happy.

On the table in the kitchen, right in the middle, was a huge box of Turkish cakes; Melba was beaming, watching my face for a reaction, and I beamed back at her.

'From my boyfriend Mehmet,' she told me happily.

'Oh, they are beautiful, marvellous.' I was not being completely honest: there were too many of them, and they were very sweet and my dentist friends have put me off sugar for life, and in any case I do not have any appetite these days. Often I get presents I do not really like, and do not know what to do about them.

'You must eat, make you strong, much food good for you.' At first Melba, who is quite a bit younger than me, called me Professor or Doctor, now she treats me like her little daughter in Colombia. I try to tell her that it is not eating that will make me strong, but being strong that will make me eat. She has great vitality and independence, is a modern person in every way, and yet says things that I thought had long gone out of fashion, such as that men don't cry, if you eat your food you become strong, and if you don't dry your hair you catch a cold.

Melba. I have been in love with three nurses and one physiotherapist, and now I am in love with Melba, who is standing fully clothed next to me, almost touching my naked skin as I recover my breath after the exertion of stripping myself. Melba. I even love her name.

'The water is good?' she asks.

I lean over the bath and dip my finger into it.

'Perfect.'

Melba, attractive, vivacious, sophisticated, and now for fixed periods every week from Monday to Friday, mine, as I am hers. We have a perfect relationship, of a kind I have never contemplated in my life and it is based on, of all things, money. I have bought happiness, for cash. She feeds me, cleans me, cheers me up, washes my clothes and makes my bed, and I pay her. It is a contract, to look after me and make me feel good; for five pounds an hour, I am purchasing and she is selling a couple of hours of her time each day (plus train fare), no sex, no personal relationship, and it is working perfectly, as if the purely legal and impersonal context enables us to have an extraordinary and immediate personal intimacy. At first I thought it was the cultural thing that was drawing me to her, her Latin American quality, so evocative of Lucia, and I am sure this is a factor, but the major point is this wonderful voluntary closeness.

Sometimes Mehmet comes to help with the cleaning, and I am always a little amazed to discover that people like themselves who probably have house-servants in their own countries, are willing to do cleaning and washing and cooking for others when studying in London. Perhaps he comes to look me over, and the cakes are a sign that I passed. I smile at myself for my dishonesty about liking them, super-truthful Albie ('he makes an absolute fetish about honesty') lying over a small thing like this.

Getting into the bath is still a cumbersome operation, but I am better at it, and really enjoy the delicious moment as the hot water creeps over my skin. Melba always leaves me to soak for a few minutes while she takes the laundry out of the washing machine. Then she returns, and I key myself up for the blissful moments.

'You are ready?'

Melba tests the water spraying out of the hand shower and begins soaping me, starting with my shoulders and working her way carefully down my back and round my chest. Lower and lower she goes, past the navel, on the bottom of my stomach, dwelling on the skin above my crotch. Then she stops.

'Now your leg . . . first the left.'

I lift my left leg, and she lays on a lather of soap round the ankle, up the calf, over my knee, along my thigh, rubbing the skin, higher and higher, spectacles . . . testicles . . . And she stops.

One day, I say to myself, one day I might react.

I am not sure whether it is better to concentrate on not displaying any physical reaction, or to think about something else.

Now my right leg, she goes very carefully around the sore on the ankle, soaps me thoroughly on the calf, all around the knee, vigorously over the slender muscles on the thigh, further and further. And stops.

It would be such an embarrassment, a violation of our impersonality, if I reacted, and yet these are not the sort of things you can control simply by effort of will. Careful, careful . . . I think I am going to make it. I wonder if she realizes that, as the saying goes, I am not unaware that she is a woman, even if to her I am just a sack of bones with operation scars and a voice.

I lean my head forward. Now, now it is coming . . .

'Aaah . . . aaah.' I do not hold back. 'Mas . . . mas . . .' I murmur. 'More . . . more . . .' This is the finest moment of the day, of the week, of the year, the one bit of unalloyed ecstasy in my life, the single blissful moment when my body forgets that it is the repository of trauma and recaptures its role as recipient if not giver of pleasure.

Thin jets of hot water spraying on my back, tickling the skin and prickling the muscles and setting my shoulders atingle with delicious liquid provocation, evokers of past delightful sensation and harbingers of future joy, may you continue to bring me bliss.

Melba. She knows how much I love the water on my back, and moves the spray from one shoulder to the other, in circles and criss-cross lines and circles again, while I wriggle my shoulder blades and contort my neck and whisper 'aah . . . aah . . . aah.'

Eventually she pulls the nozzle away from my back

and flushes the soap off my neck and shoulders, then down my chest, lovely, but nothing like on the back, under my arms, across my stomach and down a little, down, down, closer and closer. And stops.

My left leg goes up, and the water jets against my toes, up the leg, front and back, a thorough cleansing, the skin is tingling, round and round the thigh, pleasantly prickling, up a bit, higher and higher. And stops.

I glance down . . . no problem.

Up goes my right leg, and the water splashes comfortingly this way and that, I have rediscovered the delights of infancy at five pounds an hour, upwards, upwards, part of me willing her not to stop. But she stops.

'Thank you,' I say, polite even in my bath.

'It was nothing,' she replies, '*nada*', and lets the handspray down. The tubing uncurls and the nozzle plunges into the soapy water, where it slides down my leg and hits my ankle.

'Oow, oow, oow,' I scream.

Melba jumps, a look of terror on her face.

'The spray,' I shout, 'it's rubbing against my sore.'

She swiftly removes the spray, and I see tears in her eyes, my pain has gone, but she is in anguish.

'You are angry with me,' she says in Spanish.

I shake my head in denial, it was an accident.

'You are angry,' she insists.

I smile at her, and say she is my friend, how can I be angry with her.

'I hurt you. You must be very angry with me.'

I see the tears filling her dark eyelashes.

'Hit me,' she pleads, 'hit me.'

My darling, I want to say, I wish to put my arm around you and hug you and kiss you on the neck, and say that you are wonderful and I love having you near and that you are helping me with your love and affection even more than with the laundry and the food, and that it is a case of good coming out of bad, that I would never have got to know you if it wasn't for the bomb . . .

'Pass me the towel,' is all I say, and begin the laborious climb out of the bath, first my backside on the plastic seat, then lifting myself on to the platform, and finally swinging my legs over on to the carpet.

Melba. She will dress me, insisting on putting on my socks, when my feet will rest on her thighs, almost touching the dark tones of her dress over her breasts, and I will say it is not necessary and feel morally uncomfortable at her subordinating herself and she will ask if she is not doing it right, and she will help me pull on my underpants and track-suit trousers, always stopping just before they are fully pulled up. When she goes, I will ask her to tell Mehmet that I was very touched by his gift, which is true, and that the cakes are lovely, which is not. In the meanwhile she is rubbing the towel over my back, dabbing me with little cotton caresses, quietly trying to make up for the pain to my ankle, while I am trying to think of a way to show my affection.

21

Roses, massed in pink and red and crimson and cerise, banks and banks of them, orange and yellow and white as far as the eye can take in, a vast unreally-real panorama stretching out in front of me, my bench framed by rising and falling creepers in a pretty confusion of tiny blossoms, at my shoulders a myriad of roselets the colour of . . . rose.

Soon I will have to make my decision, and I know it will be an important one with a big effect on my future, but in the meanwhile I will just lean back on my bench and enjoy my first session out in the sun. I was reluctant to leave the flat when Johnny's companion suggested we all go to the Rose Garden in Regent's Park, but could not find any convincing reason for refusing her suggestion. I put on the bright green track-suit that Margit bought me, a glowing spring colour, and shuffled my way through the crowd milling around the entrance to the garden. Johnny and Lucia (yes, she is also called Lucia) went walking arm in arm into the heart of the display, leaving me at my request for my first session sitting solo on a public park bench.

I am still not quite used to the idea of getting into a car and going to a beauty spot. In Cape Town, at least in the parts where I was privileged to live, the beauty was everywhere, you just had to choose whether you wanted beach or mountain or both. The car was important if you wanted scones and cream, not for taking you to a place of beauty. Still, this is London, and beauty is organized like everything else, and here I am enjoying one of the wonders of the world, the massed display of early summer English roses in this lovely English park in the heart of London. The sun is not strong, but it is warming me up, and giving a bright tint to the petals, highlighting the shadings in the compact masses of colours, streaks of white in the pinks, traces of pale red in the scarlet, splashes of ochre in the orange. Children are running around on the pieces of lawn between the rosebeds, hidden by the bushes as their parents chase after them. There are many cameras – beauty cannot just be experienced, it has to be captured (we never took cameras up the mountain) – and a large number of the visitors appear to be Japanese, moving in their quiet and unobtrusive tourist way. Everyone is relaxed, ambling slowly, submitting to the splendour of the garden, a public communion of private pleasure, and no one seems to be looking at me.

Just sitting is interesting and boring. I feel strange in the outdoors, unaccustomed to dealing with all the sounds, movements and colours. I am not resting, this is a difficult encounter with the public, yet I am not doing anything, just having an experience. The problem is . . .

The problem is whether I should take my track-suit top off. I am getting really warm, almost uncomfortable, and would love to feel sunlight on my wounded skin. But my arm is chopped off and ugly. I think that, for my own part, I do not mind; let the people stare, I can take that. My body is what it is and I am not going to put it in hiding. People do notice when I pass that there is something wrong, something awry – oh yes, there is no arm sticking out of one sleeve. They do not stop and stare or say anything, but they are aware, that much I can detect. (I recall my ANC comrade Manghezi describing his first day journeying in a Copenhagen bus, and a child pointing to him and the mother telling the child to shut up, and remember the black South African nurse describing her blood being tested in a Frankfurt clinic – the whole waiting room stared at the tube expecting the bubbles to go down instead of up.) Only the children look directly at my arm, to the embarrassment of their parents and to my amusement; I want to talk to them, to tell them what happened, I am sure that rather than be horrified they

112

will be enthralled, as, perhaps in a childish way, I am. My slow walk when I entered the garden, my stick, my short-cropped hair, all identified me as an invalid, and made the picture easier for the general passer-by to assimilate. When I am sitting down it is more complex. I am just another person resting quietly on a bench, not an evident convalescent, and the surprise caused by the sight of the missing limb is all the greater.

The question, then, is not how I will feel, but how the visitors to the garden will feel. They have come here to look at beautiful things, not at mutilated limbs, they have a right to enjoy visual tranquillity and not be confronted by ugliness. This is my difficulty, whether I have the right to impose the image of my truncated arm on people who have chosen to spend their afternoon looking at roses.

On the one hand . . . on the other . . . Am I concocting yet another dilemma for myself? I think not. This is a real problem that I have to sort out for myself and develop an inner conviction as to what is the right thing. It involves my whole relation to the world outside, to others, to the public, and I must get it right and do so on my own. When I came out today, I thought I would be looking at roses and never imagined I would be making a decision with such major implications for my re-integration into the world. Perhaps all important moments are like that, they happen upon you and you have to respond unprepared. The issue is not so much of being disabled as of being disfigured and I must work out how much sensitivity I should have in respect of the discomfort my appearance causes to others.

Should I or shouldn't I? You cannot half take your top off, you either do or you don't. I could postpone the decision until I am stronger and have had more experience of being in public. Yet the issue will be the same; it is basically a moral one, of what I think of myself, and has nothing to do with experience. This intense self-consciousness, the thinking about thinking, makes me uneasy. I am pondering not the decision itself, but how to take the decision. Is it my brain or my will or my whole body that makes the choice?

Suddenly I know what my approach is going to be, and why. It is not a result of thinking the matter through, but of ceasing to think and allowing an intuitive certainty, timid but sure, to take over, a feeling that corresponds to the totality of impulse involving my will and body and brain, but not dependent on any of them, a conjunction of past experience and emotion and thought but not weighed and mixed as ingredients, just felt as a single conviction.

I lean forward a little, and pull the collar of my top up over my head. Then I manoeuvre my short right arm out of the rolled-up sleeve, and tug at the bottom of the garment until I have pulled the whole right side over the top of my head. That leaves my left arm still in the sleeve; I put the cuff in my teeth and jerk the sleeve over my hand, feeling instant relief at being cooler and pleasure at the idea of sun on my skin. The singlet which I am wearing under my top covers most of the wounds, and the visible part of my skin is pale and scarred like a roadmap. I fold the top and place it behind me to give some support to my back, conscious of the fact that the parts where my skin was sewn over at the end of my short arm are exposed and not handsome.

I settle back on the bench, enjoying the slow sensuality of the sun prickling my skin. People are walking by as before, not paying any more or less attention to me. Most are Japanese and it is not easy for me to read their faces, not because they are inscrutable, but because they are so polite. An elderly couple is approaching, by their appearance English. Will they sit on the bench next to me? They come closer and closer and sit down, continuing a conversation they were engaged in when I first sighted them. I know they have seen my arm, but it does not seem to be bothering them very much. I close my eyes and allow myself to drift into daydreaming. My intuition was right. If in my heart I feel diminished and ashamed, I will betray this in my movements and physical attitude; if I feel proud and comfortable with my reality, I will bear myself accordingly, and the world will take its cue. Victory, I have crossed the bridge, and what gives me special pleasure is that I have taken perhaps the most critical single decision of my life surrounded by roses.

22

Zuma was laughing as he received me into his arms at the front door, while comrade John had grave, sad eyes despite my exclamation of pleasure on greeting them; I have become quite expert at embraces, at welcoming with my left arm and giving a little twist to my body so as to protect the injured right side. Leaders, friends, comrades, I do not know which comes first, I am happy to have them with me, and it will also give me the chance to ask them directly about something that, if I was not sick already, I would say has been driving me sick with worry.

My question can wait, now is the moment for me to describe 'what happened'. Often when African comrades are telling a story I feel very 'white' and inhibited, lacking in laughter and impatient to hear the story's end, as if what matters is the piece of factual information being conveyed and not the savour of the telling and the rich personal interactions involved in the narrative. Yet today I know that I will relate the story well, African-style, no hurry, emphasis on the concrete little episodes that illuminate the multi-faceted relationships involved, detailing the humour, irony and human quirks, a slow progression building up the narrative so that its denouement is fully prepared and yet filled with interest and surprise. There are times for solemnity, times for earnestness, times for passionate calls to battle, and times for laughter. This is a time for laughter, the listener participating in the story by means of almost continuous and celebratory laughter. I will enjoy doing the narration and Zuma will get pleasure from egging me on to even richer and more comic concreteness, counterpointing my reportage with a melodic accompaniment of rising and falling laughter. Zuma's smile and good humour are famous, he even claims that a police spy gave himself up when he saw Zuma smiling at him. John Nkadimeng, trade unionist since my father's day, he has known me since I was a child, I want him to celebrate my survival with me, the arm is a detail, not the main thing, though I must remember that he himself lost one of his sons to a similar bomb blast, and perhaps I remind him of his slain child.

As I launch into my story, Zuma sits close by and watches me intently, ready to respond with warm chuckles and vigorous swings and shakes of his body to each statement I make. When I describe how, lying

116

on the ground in Julius Nyerere Avenue, I shouted ('but politely') in English and Portuguese he almost falls off the chair. He knows that area well, for ten years he was one of our leaders in Maputo, most of the time he was our 'Chief Rep' there, and the discussions we had over the years were extremely rewarding, and always filled with humour; the bomb that got me could well have been introduced into the country to kill him, only he was withdrawn just over a year ago and I stayed on. I start describing the part when I thought I was fighting for my life against kidnappers from Pretoria when really I was making a few feeble flaps with my shoulders against my Mozambican rescuers, and he lets out roars of supportive laughter, not waiting to the end of the sentence but, as if to underline and share with me the poignant hilarity of the situation, accompanying the climax of my words with happy explosive gurgles. I look across at comrade John, trying to force him with my vivacity to join in the mirth, but he stares back at me with sad, moist eyes. I cannot reqiure him to laugh, and yet in my soul I agree with Zuma; the situation was truly comic, we human beings really get up to the most astonishing things. Wait till I reach the Himie Cohen falling off the bus part, surely comrade John will respond then, and if Zuma is collapsing off his chair with laughter now, what will he be like when I actually tell the joke within a joke part?

Slowly I take Zuma through the hospital portion of the story, of hearing Ivo Garrido's voice and his exquisitely polite word for the state of my arm (huge laughter) and then his statement about operating and my having to face the future with courage (quieter laughter this time), and my comment at the relief I felt at being in the hands of Frelimo (appreciative laughter, high marks for being a good comrade at all times and for telling the story in a gracious and non-boastful way).

I pause so as to give space for the Himie Cohen joke, where the story will resolve itself in genuine euphoric comedy. I wonder if Zuma has heard it already, I suspect that it has done the rounds in ANC circles, though in the rather reduced form of: 'And the first thing comrade Albie did in the hospital was feel for his balls.' People have difficulty remembering the spectacles, testicles part; even Wolfie, whose cultural background is the same as mine, asked me to repeat it three times so that he could write it down correctly.

Looking directly at Zuma's smiling face, and swinging round from time to time to confront comrade John with the humour of my story, I launch into the final portion. '. . . what do you mean, Catholic? . . . spectacles, testicles, wallet and watch.' Zuma doubles up and yells with laughter, his mouth wide open, his head rolling back and then coming down again, his eyes full of sympathetic mirth. I feel moved by the situation, by the intense interaction between us. This is what the ANC is, we do not wipe out our personalities and cultures when we become members, rather we bring in and share what we have, Zuma's African-ness, his Zulu appreciation of conversation and humour is mingling with my Jewish joke, enriching it, prolonging and intensifying the pleasure. We are comrades and we are close, yet we do not have to become like each other, erase our personal tastes and ways of seeing and doing things, but rather contribute our different cultural inputs so as to give more texture to the whole. This is how one day we will rebuild South Africa, not by pushing a steamroller over the national cultures, but by bringing them together, seeing them as the many roots of a single tree, some more substantial than others, but all contributing to the tree's strength and beauty.

How many times have I not been asked why I, a white, am in a black movement, or, put another way, why I am fighting for the blacks. For years I knew there was something wrong with the question, but did not know precisely what, and it took a fortuitous statement by a teenage boy at a meeting in the USA to unlock the puzzle for me – he said his friends were arguing that the trouble with people like me was that we were always fighting to liberate others, never to liberate ourselves, was that true? I knew what he was getting at, that we should concentrate on opening up our own heads instead of running away from our personal oppression (spiritual, psychological) and becoming surrogate liberators of others. Maybe that was true of some of the middle-class protesters in the USA, though I preferred to take people at face value and not always look for hidden motives; even reactionaries could be just that, reactionaries. The fact was that it simply did not correspond to the kind of people we were in the South African struggle, where the issues were so real and entered directly into our lives – would one say that the resistance fighters against the Nazi occupation (to take the heroes of my childhood) were simply acting out their own problems? But this young guy had a point and it was a fundamental one: we were not fighting to free someone else, we were in fact fighting for ourselves, we were struggling for our own rights, the right to be free citizens of a free country, that was the answer, and the only way we could achieve our own true freedom was by helping to destroy the system of white domination that was crushing the whole country and denying us all our humanity, black and white.

Am I being looked after, do I have any problems?

I assure them that in my daily life I am being beautifully cared for and that the International Defence and Aid Fund is helping out with all expenses, including transport to the physiotherapy gym three mornings a week and the costs of the prosthesis, while the ANC office in London has kept constantly in touch, so that now it is really up to me and no one else.

Now it is Zuma's turn; just as some people bring me cherries or flowers or chocolates, he offers me his gift, some choice political information. It is about the negotiations over the withdrawal of South African troops from Angola and the independence of Namibia – like old times in Maputo, he is giving a briefing session, and comrade John chips in from time to time. It seems that the negotiations have to be taken very seriously and will probably succeed . . . they represent a victory for the peoples of Angola and Namibia, and we have to keep one step ahead . . . we have started moving our people already from Angola, we don't want to hang on until the last minute and allow a difficult situation to arise . . .

I am not quite ready yet for global and regional politics, that will come back with my general recovery, but I appreciate the gesture in keeping me informed, and feel that the moment has arrived for me to raise what is on my mind.

'I, er . . . wonder if this is a good moment to ask, but there's something that's been worrying me for some time,' I start off hesitantly. 'It's about items that have appeared in the press . . .' I think they know what I am going to ask, but they wait patiently for me to put my question.

'There was a report in *The Times* that some of our leading comrades connected with military actions had said that the time had come to hit white civilian targets so as to show the white population that their government couldn't protect them . . .' I want to speak slowly and naturally, as though this is just another item that has popped up in our conversation, but I am tense and the words come out in a staccato but endless flow. Bombs have been going off in rubbish trays, outside the Ellis Park sports stadium, there is talk of the 'Ellis Park tendency' in the ANC, bombs, bombs and more bombs, that is part of the struggle, but are they just being let off anywhere, are we entering an endless Northern Ireland or Lebanon type of situation, where the action becomes everything and politics get left behind? Am I reacting as a white, more concerned about the way such a campaign would block the growing breakthrough of our ideas into the white community, so that all the leading writers and most of the intelligentsia in general, churchpeople, students, many university lecturers and schoolteachers were now with us (while, I sometimes joked, all the journalists were either with us or with the security police, those with us pretending to be with the security police and those with the security police pretending to be with us)? It is not just that, and it is certainly not just the negative effect it would have on our international reputation – I do not think we should do and not do things because of what people think of us. No, the worry is over what the implications might be for the morale and political consciousness of our fighters, their impatience with the new complicated phase our struggle is in.

If I were out and about, I would be joining in the debate, making my points through our structures, listening to other arguments, taking the issue as just another one of the important questions our movement is faced with from time to time. In fact I am sitting around on my own all the time, thinking about my own problems, in a highly subjective frame of mind, and all the while worrying about whether we are in danger of becoming not much different from the other side, except that we have historic justice with us and they do not. In particular, and this is what I dare not say to Zuma and comrade John, I can take the loss of my arm if we are involved in a liberation struggle, and do so with pride, but if we are just going for civilians as a matter of policy, what was it all for?

I limit my question to the newspaper report: is it accurate and does it represent a new policy in the ANC?

Zuma looks at comrade John, comrade John looks at Zuma. It is Zuma, my 'Chief Rep' who speaks.

It is true that interviews were given to the press and that they have given rise to a great deal of discussion in the organization, he informs me, speaking with gravity and deliberation, almost as if giving a press interview. Recently the full National Executive Committee met, including all the persons who had given interviews, and the matter was fully debated. 'The result,' he says, choosing his words carefully, 'is that the NEC fully reaffirmed that ANC policy was not to go for civilian targets, and any statements made to the contrary were repudiated as being against our policy.'

I want to jump up and embrace him, not because I do not have any sympathy for the combatants who are risking everything each day and who are filled with anger at the cruelty of the regime and eager to use all the resources at their command, but because the issue has been tackled through discussion and argument, with everybody having a chance to put their positions, and what I would have thought to be the correct decision was taken in a democratic way, so that it is not just 'the line' being thrust down the throats of everybody,

122

but the thoroughly debated decision of the leadership arrived at after full discussion.

Perhaps it is time to return the conversation to lighter themes; this topic is a tricky one.

'There's just one request I would like to make of you,' I say, smiling a little. They nod.

'I received a lovely note from OR,' I continue, using the affectionate reference to the first name initials of our President, Oliver Tambo, 'and I was very moved by it, but he thanks me for the message I sent just after the explosion . . . the fact is I have no recollection at all of having sent any message.'

Zuma is looking at me with a smile ready to break out on his face.

'I wonder,' I continue, 'if you could check on the files and let me know one day what it was I said?'

Zuma roars with laughter, and the tension is over. I sneak a glance at comrade John, but he still looks sad; this is one battle I have lost.

'I am obviously very militant when I am concussed,' I add, amused by the idea, but still comrade John does not laugh.

23

I take the black canvas bag out of the cupboard, my favourite carrier for hand luggage, place it on the carpet near my bed, grip the top of the bag with my teeth, pull the zip open with my left hand, and take out my arm. Some lines of Thomas Hood come back to me:

A cannon-ball took off his legs,
So he laid down his arms.

This combination of plastic and metal and leather, waiting for me to give it life, is my arm, this hollowed flesh-coloured (white male) material, the top section shaped to fit snugly on my shoulder, curving and swollen in the middle to give the appearance of biceps, the bottom part joined on by a hinge at elbow height and shaped like a forearm, with a metal plate at the end capable of receiving any fitting such as a split hook or a hand.

My hand. I do not even know where I put it, it has been beautifully shaped, the fingers carefully measured, and I suppose if I wanted to I could pretend it was my hand, the engineer even chose a tone half-way between winter paleness and summer tan. It lies in a cupboard somewhere, ready to frighten an unsuspecting burglar one day. A hand feels, it touches, you stroke things with a hand, make love, tickle the most secret and sensitive parts of another with it, you greet strangers and friends, negotiate and feel your way through the world with your hand. Your hand is your imagination, your instinct, it contains your anger and your love, it does not pretend to be a hand, it is a hand. No one spoke to me about these things. The engineer was sympathetic and sensitive, he takes great pride in his work, in turning out a product that is functional, elegant and in keeping as far as possible with the wishes of the client. The problem is that the client, that is, me, did not really know what his wishes were; it was not basically a technical problem, like choosing shoes that fitted and looked good, nor simply a subjective question, like deciding on an ice cream flavour. In fact, only now do I feel that I am really beginning to discern what the real motive is that lies behind the strong desire for me to wear and love my prosthesis.

The specialists were delighted with me at first when I appeared at the limb-fitting unit to try on my arm, I was joking and enthusiastic, eager to collaborate, submitting to measurements and fittings as though I were trying on a suit for my wedding-day (will I ever marry again?). I did all the exercises I was asked to do, lifting pegs from holes and then putting them back again, confident that with practice I would learn to wear the prosthesis as easily as I had learnt to write with my left hand. Now they get irritated when I come because I theorize so much, clearly they would prefer me to make up my mind and then shut up: either wear the damned thing, or leave it alone, but not go on and on with my explanations as to why it is proving so difficult for me.

I slip my short arm into the shoulder holster, feeling the coolness of the plastic on my skin. I have to wriggle the flesh and muscles a bit to get a snug fit, and as I do so the nerves tingle with a phantom pins-and-needles sensation. I straighten the lower portion so that it is pointing in front of me and then begin adjusting the harness behind my back, stretching and stretching until I feel the buckle is in position. Now I pull the strap at the end under my left shoulder and thread it through the clasp: one, two three holes, four, five, that's it to get just the right tension.

Very early on in hospital, when I was short of breath, and knew there was something wrong with my brain because the intellectual content of Dallas was too much for me, and I could only take quizzes and game-shows, I saw something unexpected and very beautiful on television. It was a children's show in the afternoon, and I was only half watching when I suddenly became aware of a man running forward and bending to scoop up a child in his left arm – he was wearing dark clothing, a suit, I think, and his right arm was missing, from the shoulder, and he held the child close to him with great tenderness, and I felt very happy to see him, he looked so spontaneous and affectionate.

Some time later Father John, the Anglican priest whose hand was blasted off when he opened a parcel destined for ANC refugees, came to see me in hospital, and the conversation went easily until I asked him about his prosthesis, and he became tense and muttered: oh that, I threw it away after one day. He told me that he could do everything with his good hand, and only asked his friends to help when it came to cutting meat. The bag of cherries which he had brought me, he added with a smile, he had carried in his teeth while in the underground. So far, the score for wearing a prosthesis was two against, nil in favour.

Then one day when I went for my training session at the upper limb unit (why not arm unit? I wondered) I was surprised to see a lady of about my age busy at an ironing board right in the middle of the training room. I looked at my watch to see if I had come too early or too late, but no, like a good member of the ANC, I was exactly on time. This seemed to be a strange moment for someone to be interrupting my session by doing staff laundry, and I peeped over to see exactly what it was that had to be ironed there and then. It was an ordinary blouse she was pressing, not hospital wear, first doing the sleeves, then the collar, then, turned around, the body of the garment. I looked about for the trainer (the seventh or eighth person with whom I had fallen in love), but she was not to be seen, so I sat down and glanced impatiently at the ironing lady, waiting for her to go away. She did not have the air of an employee, in fact she was wearing elegant outdoor rather than working clothes, and then, of course, it came to me, her right hand was artificial. Seeing me looking in her direction, she started talking to me in a soft, cultivated voice, something about the weather, and I felt with a certain measure of pleasure that she and I belonged to the great democracy of the disabled, and as such were able to communicate easily with each other. Soon we were on to the question of her prosthesis, a battery-operated below-elbow upper-limb fitting, to give it its full title, and she was telling me that she was very happy with it, and I could see that this was so. Hang on in there, she told me in her quiet voice (so she knew my problem, and had been asked to give me a demonstration, never mind). Now the score was two-one, except that just before she left she confided something to me that made me wonder again: her biggest nightmare was that her friends would appear suddenly at the door and catch her without her prosthesis. Oh no, I thought to myself, never, never.

I have been trying to work out the circumstances when I would want to wear my prosthesis. I certainly do not require it for cosmetic reasons, though I can understand that for other people this would be fundamental, I actually find it anti-cosmetic, and could not bear to be frightened that I would be caught without it, or that someone will shake my hand and discover that it is made of plastic. The one clear case of where I thought it might be useful would be for driving.

I telephoned a man who had been to the limb-fitting unit to have a special adjustment made to his prosthesis to help him play better golf. His secretary wanted to know what it was about, and I felt reluctant to say it was about our arms, so I just stated it was a personal matter. Eventually I got through to him, and he told me straight away about all the sports he had played, football, cricket and now golf and he was also a keen swimmer, as if that was what really mattered. I suppose having been able to do all these things as a youth meant that they were not so important to me now. What I wanted to know was did he feel like a freak, how was it when he made love, do his friends always identify him as the one-armed bandit or do they see him as him? But somehow these are not the subjects one discusses at the limb-training centre, nor on the telephone, one talks about practical and technical questions only. So I asked him if he wore his prosthesis all the time, and he said yes, he had it on then. Was it useful? Not really, he answered, except to hold paper down. So it was really just cosmetic? Yes, except when he played sports, then he put on special fittings, oh, and just one thing, he never wore his prosthesis when driving.

I was not quite sure how to score this one but gave the benefit of the doubt to the prosthesis. Two-two.

It was then that I saw Tommy's mother, by mistake (or was it?). Tommy was a little kid who was playing with plasticine when I arrived at the training centre. His arms were tiny little protuberances which he used most skilfully to manipulate the plasticine while he chattered away cheerfully and non-stop with a strong Inner London accent. At one stage he got up to fetch a toy telephone, and I saw as he hobbled along that both his legs were artificial. Soon we were having an imaginary conversation on the phone, shouting to each other across the room. I liked him, he was outgoing and full of a mischievous kind of fun. And then his mother walked in. Her hair was swept up, and she had a stylish, short-sleeved summer dress on, and as she strode gracefully to the middle of the room and took command of her little boy I became aware that she was lovely, had the proud carriage of a London working-class woman aware of her beauty, and that one arm was missing, or, rather, she had a very short arm. (I refused even in my mind to say short stump, got into trouble with the engineer over this, he said it was the scientific word, I said that may be so, but it was my short arm, not my stump, and I was irritable when I said this, just as the psychiatrist had warned I might be.) I looked at the way she bore herself, her conviction and sparkle, and said to myself: yes, yes, yes, that's what I want to be like. So now it was three-two against, but Tommy's mother had really decided the matter for me once and for all.

By now I think I have come to realize why wearing or not wearing a prosthesis arouses such strong emotion, and why I get so tense and irritable on the subject. It is a question not of science or medicine but of magic, of how we deal with fate. I am not speaking about lower limbs (legs) or cases where both hands are lost. I am sure that in either of these situations prostheses are immensely practical things, enabling one to walk or write or to clean and dress oneself. But in my case, I can do all these things quite comfortably, and the prosthesis in fact has little functional value. At the same time I do not want to hide from anyone the fact that I have lost my arm – on the contrary, in certain circumstances it could actually be functional for people to know, so that they can make simple adjustments, like when shaking my hand, or helping with doors, or cutting meat when needed. The reality is that everyone wants me to be given my arm back, we cannot stand the idea of a physical mutilation that is so evident and such an affront, we want the effects of the blast to be wiped out. My friends and comrades and family desire deeply that I have a substitute arm so that the constant reminder of my loss can be eliminated, so that I can be normalized again. Science, will-power and training are the ingredients of the magic potion that will make my arm grow again. I too believed in this at an earlier stage, that I would get an artificial arm that would work so well that no one would notice the difference, this being the real test, how normal it made me look. But now I think differently. I can make up for the loss to a large extent by developing skills in my left hand, using my teeth and knees and forehead and feet when appropriate, getting specially designed instruments, avoiding physically stressful situations, getting help from friends – I could answer a whole exam question on the point. Then there are circumstances where I just have to acknowledge that there are things I can no longer do. The crucial question is: do I feel more comfortable in the world, more myself, with or without a prosthesis?

I promised myself that I would wear the prosthesis for two weeks, with the right to take two days off during this period. I am pleased that this is the last day and that I will soon be released from my undertaking. It is not uncomfortable, nor specially comfortable. The split hook protrudes from the end, ready to be opened by a movement of my left shoulder-blade, which tightens the harness and pulls on a leather thong attached to one prong of the hook. The engineer insists that in his experience this muscle-operated prosthesis is far more efficient and comfortable than the battery-operated one – the latter works on the basis of skin tone caused by certain movements of the arm activating cells which in turn cause fingers on a plastic hand-substitute to open and shut, it is heavy and causes more frustration than it is worth to the wearers. In some cases of below-elbow amputees and just a very few above-elbow cases, the cell-operated prosthesis works well, but he personally recommends the muscle-operated one, though it is always the patient who chooses.

For two months now I have been struggling with the arm, getting depressed and irritable every time I put it on. My psychiatrist, who generously comes to see me where I am staying, has warned me that it was difficult learning to live without an arm, now it will be difficult learning to live with one again. He was right, the whole subject causes me so much discomfort that I wish it would simply vanish. One day somebody was visiting and placed a canvas carry-on bag right next to the one with my arm in it. I laughed to myself as I imagined this person taking the wrong bag home by mistake, opening it and discovering . . . If only something like that would happen.

I adjust the angle of the lower part of the prosthesis by pulling on the strap to release a catch, twist the split hook into the most convenient position, and begin my activities for the day. What has undermined me completely is the knowledge that the prosthesis will not actually help me with a single one of my tasks, that I will be wearing it simply to give the appearance of having an arm. Perhaps the training should have been more geared to real-life situations where I would actually have required the assistance of a second arm, that is, to use the terminology, where I would have had to be bilateral. The reality is that I have strapped the prosthesis on for the sake of my honour, so that

I can say to anyone who asks me that I really gave it a try. Maybe after six months or a year, when I am feeling physically much stronger and generally more integrated into the world, I can come back to it, now I am just counting the hours till I can take it off, put it back in the canvas bag, and then shove the bag in a cupboard for a good long time. One theory is that it is always better to wait till the patient is fully recovered from all other aspects of the trauma before fitting the limb, the other is to begin as soon as possible. I was in a hurry, and I have failed.

The only moral consolation I get is that one day I will write this all down, so that other trainers and amputees might benefit. The most important thing is to have a counsellor right from the start who looks at the problem as a whole and understands the meaning of an arm to a patient and the difference between an arm that feels and has sensation and loves, and an instrument that looks like an arm and is capable of performing some of the functions of an arm. Then the patient should be given all the information necessary for exercising options. Patients should be given every encouragement to try the prosthesis, but advised right from the beginning that there is no question of moral success or failure involved one way or the other, it is a very intimate and personal thing that will vary from individual to individual, what matters is that everyone should know the options and give them a reasonable try before determining which one suits him or her best.

In the meantime, for all my theorizing and analysis, I feel a failure. Someone said I should wear the prosthesis for the ANC, and I responded sharply that if I wore the arm, it would be for me and not for the ANC, and then if I were happy and functioning well, that is what would be good for the ANC. I know that I will not wear the arm again, and that the vision that dominates me completely is that of Tommy's mother walking proudly, graciously and beautifully in the world, short arm exposed, as she is (it never stopped the men, she told my friend). Yet however hard I try, I cannot get rid of the feeling that I have badly let myself down, and the ANC too.

24

The bench seems far too steep. I would hate to fall in front of the camera that is tracking me as I slowly edge my way, foot by foot, up the incline. The physiotherapist holds my hand until I am right above her when she lets go and stands aside. I am perched high up on my own, left arm outstretched, my short right arm wobbling to help me keep my balance, looking down on the heads of the camera crew and director as I shuffle closer to the wall bars. I wish she had not walked away, but had kept her arm outstretched so as to leave her fingers nearly touching mine, ballet-like and visually far more interesting, evocative of the nearly-touching fingers of Michelangelo's floating bodies of Adam and the Lord.

The gym is filled with patients exercising their legs, bending, stretching, flexing and retracting knees and ankles and toes in endlessly boring but necessary repetitions. In the discreet way the English have of looking without looking, they are accompanying my slow progress up the bench that is hooked at a steep angle to the bars, no doubt wondering, as I am, whether I am going to topple off. The presence of the BBC film-makers does something to all of us, we exercise a little more enthusiastically and self-consciously, pat our hair into place, straighten our clothing, even when the camera is not pointing in our direction.

There are little bumps on the bench near the top of the incline, and I am eager to feel them underfoot because then I will be far up enough to grasp one of the bars, turn around and begin the descent. My toes inch forward . . . not yet, then the other foot . . . ah, at last I can feel the unevenness under my sole, now is the moment to lurch forward, an instant of panic as my posture shifts, then sharp relief as I grab the wooden bar, breathing heavily, my head up in the air. There is no need for me to invent intense concentration, to simulate strain and effort. When the BBC asked if I would grant them an interview, I accepted happily, and we agreed that it would be useful to film me during one of my sessions in the physio gym. I turn around carefully, twisting the balls of my feet so that they face downwards, and direct my fingers to leave go of the bar. Once more, that moment of total fear as, unsupported, I swing round and adjust my balance, panicky that I will crash down to the floorboards. The bumps are now under my heels, and I begin my descent, moving even more slowly and cautiously, waiting anxiously for the moment when the physio takes my hand in hers again. Left foot, right foot, I feel I should not be so hunched, but am afraid to straighten up, her hand is almost touching, I must keep going steadily, now she is touching and holding me, I am a little child on a swing, and I want to run the last few paces down, but hold myself in, move down slowly and step off triumphantly, smiling.

Would you mind very much doing it again? the director asks, we got your bodies and faces, this time we would like to get your feet. And, by the way, he adds to the physio, can you keep your hand outstretched after letting go of Albie, it shows the relationship between you?

Delighted at his vindication of my directorial eye, I begin the slow ascent once more. Film-making fascinates me; my first activity outside hospital was completing the film that Sol, my Mozambican friend, and Margit and I had been making on how Mozambican artists were responding to the war which engulfs their country. I wrote books on the murals of Maputo and the Children's Dance School, in which, with Alvin Ailey posters in the background, black and white kids could be seen doing classical ballet, modern dance and the dances of Africa. Nothing would delight me more than to do law part-time and concentrate on making films and encouraging art and creating opportunities for concerts and dance. Southern Africa is potentially one of the great zones of cultural creativity in the world; we have a rare combination of a popular culture still deeply rooted and vigorous amongst the people and the dynamism of modern industrial life, and I sometimes have visions of helping to organize great cultural festivals to celebrate our freedom in a new South Africa, a giant carnival through the streets of Cape Town, a jazz jamboree in Ellis Park. I used to argue that culture was an instrument of struggle, that the artist should be committed, et cetera, but now I see culture as something much deeper, more profound, an expression of what we are and what we are becoming, and the artist as someone naturally engaged with life, including struggle, rather than a person trying consciously to fashion knives or

135

bullets with words or pictures or sound. Our commitment is spontaneous, uneven, maddening, personal and all the richer for that. My softness presupposes hardness in others. Long may we clash and enjoy each other. My toes are tickling as they know they are being filmed, I must be careful not to daydream too much while I make my way slowly up the bench. My arm is stretched wide, hand resting on the hand of the physio, my feet are moving one in front of the other and I am keeping fairly upright. Gradually as I ascend my fingers slide free, while those of the physio remain poised almost touching. My feet encounter the bumps, I turn around carefully, begin the descent and float my hand down until it gently cradles itself in that of the physio once more, and she graciously escorts me as if in a minuet down to the ground.

Lovely, lovely, says the director, now I wonder if you could do it just one more time while we film you from a distance or would that be a terrible bore?

The fact is that I love being filmed, it is as if the camera is healing me by recording my image, counteracting the terrible hatred contained in the bomb, declaring implicitly that I must be a worthwhile person, otherwise why would respectable people like the BBC bother to film me? This is my vengeance, my way of fighting back, not by killing others, but by transmuting bad into good, using my heart and brains to project as much as possible a vision of survival, struggle, triumph and humanity. In American terms some would regard me as a wimp, what I liked about George Bush was exactly his wimpishness (wimpicity), in British language I would be a wet, and what I look forward to is the day when the wimps and the wets and the weak inherit the earth, boys and girls alike. There are enough of us, and the rough, tough guys, always in command of themselves and others, have not done too good a job with all their power.

The first interview I gave came out even better than I had hoped for, a sympathetic spread in the *New York Times* under the sub-heading: 'Broken but unbroken'. Lucia taught me sharply in relation to love and personal relationships not to have the psychology of a victim, and now I am extending this principle to my post-bomb situation. I am not a victim seeking revenge or compensation or sympathy, but someone who voluntarily engaged himself in a freedom struggle, aware that risks at some stage or the other were involved, delighted that I have survived and determined to re-establish an active and happy relationship with the world. Then came interviews in the London *Observer*, the *Catholic Herald*, the *Morning Star*, the BBC Africa Service, quite a wide spread ideologically, but all treating me as I was hoping they would, emphasizing softness and humour and quiet resilience rather than flag-waving toughness. I grumbled about these interviews, and when asked if I was in hiding in London answered: yes, but not from my enemies, from my friends, I just can't cope. Yet in a way that almost alarms me, I feel myself being re-legitimized by the media, the near-alarm coming from the dependence I feel on them for creating a warm and sympathetic image of me. Virtually my first steps out of doors were captured by Independent Television newscasters who showed me in a track-suit treading gently on lawn, surrounded by flowers, as though I had come twice out of hospital, once to this tucked-away garden flat and once on to the TV screen where my friends could see me. Something I liked very much, and it came as a bit of a surprise, was the delicacy and warmth with which the journalists treated me, not only during interviews but afterwards, the *Morning Star* photographer sending me soft and cheerful portraits that he had taken, and a large group of journalists on the *Observer* clubbing together to buy me a selection of thirty or more compact discs, Mozart, Schubert, Beethoven, Mahler, lots of my favourites; everyone continues to tell me that Britain has become a harder, loads-a-money society, and I am sure that they are right, but I am also being constantly reminded of another Britain that is aglow and spontaneously generous, and I am not going to deny myself the pleasure of feeling and enjoying its warmth and human solidarity.

The filming continues for half an hour while I ride an exercise bicycle, lean backwards over a large, brightly coloured ball, balance on wobble boards, and try to walk swiftly in a straight line.

A second physio, who looked after me with great affection and dedication when I first came to the gym, and who has now gone upstairs to backs or hips or noses or something, comes down specially to be in the film and asks me with friendly provocation how many sit-ups I can do now. Let's see, I answer. She sits firmly on my feet, and holds my thighs while I pull my trunk up, further and further until my nose is touching her shoulder. In my memory she is Ms Littlemore because she is always saying: just a little more, just a little more. My feet feel comfortable under her buttocks, and I enjoy the sense that she is committing herself not just with words but with the weight of her body to my recovery, a physical giving of herself in a professional setting that I always find moving. Two pull-ups, three, four, five, so far it is going easily, eight, nine, ten, what the director wants is the part where I am really straining, I must think of something else, anything else, we always spend our lives thinking of something else . . . the sensitive interview with the man from the *Guardian*, he wanted to know about my youth, how I first got involved, and I told him I distanced myself from my parents' politics, I was a little green because it was non-confrontational, it was easier to save trees than people . . . I am not there yet, seventeen, eighteen, nineteen, now I'm beginning to struggle . . . then we had to make choices. It was not about apartheid, but about whether a date on a Saturday night and a box of sticky chocolates in a hot cinema was what life was about. I met a young crowd with other ideas, musical evenings, all-night parties and walking home afterwards, we climbed the mountain, argued about everything, even our arguments, and that was how it all began. If you judge the accomplishment of an organization by the number of years its members later spent in prison, we were the most likely to succeed, and succeed we did . . . twenty-three, twenty-four, I do not think I can manage any more, I must try one last one. I clamp my jaws, contort my face, and slowly lever my trunk upwards, come on, just a little more, just a little more, she urges, and I almost start smiling and break my weightlifter-like concentration, but manage to maintain my rigidity and with a last spurt of energy, succeed in pulling myself up to her shoulder. A big smile spreads over my face and I flop backwards, exhausted but happy that I made the nice round number of twenty-five.

The whole process of being filmed somehow contributes in a small way to the reconstruction of my self. In a short sad letter to me, Lucia, after mentioning a series of ridiculous impediments to her and the man she loves getting married, says she does not like my letters because they are too narcissistic. In part she is right, but I have to attend in my own way to the question of image. The public, or at least that section which is interested, has a picture of me as a blast victim, in fact a photograph was taken of me moments after the explosion and it appeared in newspapers all over the world, showing me lying on the ground, trying to lift my trunk up, and I have to try now to controvert that terrible image (which I can barely look at, and even less the TV images of my body being dragged away). That is why I like pictures of me smiling or writing or doing exercises, I do not want people associating me with violence and horror but with regrowth and happiness, with the quiet victory of recovery.

25

Melba is standing next to the bath, holding my out-stretched hand and weeping. She is not even looking at me, but staring straight ahead and talking rapidly as the drops fill her dark lashes. From the moment when she burst in through the front door and began sorting the clothes and organizing the kitchen I could see that she lacked her usual cheeriness.

'I have never met anyone like you before,' she says, struggling to get the words out. She is speaking Spanish and I have to concentrate with all my will not to miss what she is saying. 'You have lost your arm and still you are fighting for human rights.'

I am stirred by her emotion, but am sitting uncomfortably, my knees peeping up from the bath bubbles, and my left arm held across my body to reach her hand. This is the first time she has taken my hand in hers, and the warmth of her grasp intensifies the sense of physical agitation and closeness. She has cut her hair and is wearing a dress that, although dark and soberly elegant, has hints of summer in it. I have been taken by surprise by her sudden speech, and feel myself thrilled by her defiance of the unwritten contract between us and uncertain about where it will lead.

'It has been very wonderful working for you these past weeks, I have never had an experience like this, you haven't changed at all, you still have all your beliefs in spite of what has happened to you . . .'

No, no, I want to interrupt, there are many problems that I still have to solve, many doubts, but I am so happy that you like me because I like you, and it is your cheerfulness and vitality that has helped me each day and enabled me to feel the savour of life, and in any case, you exaggerate, because there are thousands and thousands like me in South Africa and Mozambique, and I am sure that in your country Colombia there are many who have fought for freedom and paid some penalty for it, only you have not met them yet.

'. . . You carry on full of good spirits, making a film, preparing to write a book,' she continues, tears on her cheeks, 'and my life is nothing, and I am not important at all . . .'

I want to protest, to intervene, but she has got my hand firmly clasped in hers and I cannot wave to her to stop.

'For the past weeks it has been terrible for me coming here, I get nervous every time I touch you . . .'

So she did feel something, I was not just a sack of bones and bruises to her, I feel exultant.

'. . . so I cannot carry on any more, today is my last day, next week my friend from Colombia will take over

141

from me, she is very good and will look after you better than I have done.'

I am disappointed by the news, downcast, but still stirred by the intensity of her feeling and full of powerful emotion myself. If I cannot leap out of the bath and embrace her, at least I would like the chance to make an emotional speech myself. Yet she keeps her face averted from me, and holds so tightly to my hand that I am kept mute.

'Melba . . .' I start, but she drops my hand, places a towel around my shoulder and dashes off to the kitchen.

I heave and lever myself out of the bath, dry my back and front and legs as well as I can, partially dress myself, and hobble along to the kitchen.

'Melba . . .' She dashes past me, grabs the Hoover and runs it noisily over the carpet. I sit down at the table and while I am eating think about what I will say.

She has finished hoovering, so I get up as rapidly as I can and move in her direction.

'Melba . . .' Mumbling that the hour is advanced, she puts the Hoover in the cupboard and rushes to my bedroom. This time I do not attempt to stumble along after her, but go back to the kitchen and eat calmly. Proceeding at an easy pace, I complete my meal and stack the plates in the sink, my one gesture to housekeeping so far. Then, walking deliberately and casually to my bedroom, I start again:

'Melba . . .'

'I have to wash the dishes,' she says in a strained voice and brushes past me.

The way things are going, I will be lucky if she stands still long enough for me to pay her. I wonder how much extra I dare think of paying her as a farewell bonus. She needs the money, yet always refuses to take anything above her per diem, insisting that I deduct for that time when she came quarter of an hour late, and I say, ah yes, but you did some shopping for me and she says, oh no, that does not count, she did it as a friend, and then I remember triumphantly that she went on a Saturday morning to book my plane ticket, but she responds by reminding me of that occasion when she left early because she had to meet someone, and I prod my brains furiously for an answer. Once Wolfie was waiting to speak to me when he heard Melba and me shouting violently at each other in Spanish. He seemed quite alarmed, everybody treated me with special delicacy, and here was this person yelling angrily at me, and maybe it would set back my recuperation. 'I . . . er . . . don't want to interfere,' he stated cautiously . . . 'It's all right, Wolfie,' I smiled at him 'we're arguing because she insists that I am paying her too much and I am sure that I am paying her too little.' I also wanted to tell him that this was a cultural thing; if we spoke in an excited way, with a lot of volume and vivacity, it did not mean we were angry, but simply that the subject was a lively one that meant something to us.

With the money counted out in my hand, I walk to the kitchen, and stand in the doorway. She is trapped. 'This is what I owe you, and this is a little extra for you to buy a present for Mehmet or your daughter.'

To my surprise, she does not object, but takes a piece of paper out of her handbag, writes something on it and puts it in my hand.

'This is my address and phone number if you ever come to Bogotá. Goodbye.'

She raises her arms, places them carefully around my shoulders so as not to hurt the still injured parts, and

143

gives me a quick farewell squeeze. This is the first time I am feeling her body pressed against mine, the softness of her bosom against my chest, the gentleness of her arms now around my waist, but before I can envelop her with my left arm and give some pressure of my own, she has pulled away, and within moments she is departing, no, fleeing, through the front door.

Adios, Melba, and whatever you say, this man is going to rest his head against a pillow and have a good cry.

26

If I was a rich man . . . Riding around in minicabs is going to my head. I have not been this poor for years, yet spending money on cabs all the time and paying someone to wash my back is giving me fantasies of being rich. My economy is upside down, I stay with friends, pay a certain amount for food, incur no entertainment expenses, so have few of the outgoings of ordinary working people. I drew half of my savings to pay for the technical upgrading of the film we made on art and war in Mozambique, and then took out the remaining half to purchase tickets for my children to visit South Africa for the first time in their lives. Now I have nothing. Friends tell me not to buy flowers, since I must save all I can, and I reply that if I were to rely on ordinary budgeting my situation would be catastrophic and I would not stand a chance. My only hope was magic, and magic needs flowers.

Luckily for me at this stage, I hate money, I hate keeping accounts, carrying cash around, and do not understand the new cards that banks are giving out, new, that is, to someone who has been away for ten years. I have virtually no pension rights and am always astonished at meeting people in their twenties already telling you what marvellous pension schemes they belong to – our pension has always been the Revolution, which perhaps has taken a little while to mature, but nevertheless has given us a sense of moral security and also the material back-up of a vast extended family. I have never worked full-time for the ANC, and have earned a modest living over the years as an advocate, law teacher and writer. I pay something towards the upkeep of my children each month, own some fine contemporary Mozambican sculpture and paintings, and that is about it.

Yet if I was a rich man . . . Samora used to complain that the reason why Mozambique with its great natural resources was so poor was that the people still had the psychology of underdevelopment; the enemy, he said, is camping in our heads. Some might say that he placed too much stress on consciousness and not enough on proper planning and the organization of efficient systems, but the fact is that he reached something in all of us, our thinking is small and parsimonious in every way, and we have to open up our heads and imaginations. Comrades bring me second-hand clothing from a thrift shop. I have no problem in wearing second-hand clothing, the idea even appeals to me, but I want it to be attractive, not just any old thing you put on because you are not allowed to go round naked. A friend who works for a Citizen's Advice Bureau tells me enthusiastically that if I fill in a series of forms I can get a disability grant. I ask how much it is, and learn that it would cover not even half of what I am spending on minicabs each week.

If I was a rich man . . . buying these little services that were always out of my range makes me wonder what it would be like to be really rich, what changes it would make in my life. I must still have the psychology of underdevelopment, all I can think of is more minicabs and perhaps more leg-space on aeroplanes. The thought of owning a vast home fills me with gloom, and the idea of having two homes doubles the sense of misery. I will never get my car back again, but when I learn to drive with one hand, the only feature that I will insist on my new car having is an automatic gear-box. Once I attended a conference in upstate New York that was catered for by a top chef, and for the first three days I could not wait for meals; then I found I could no longer bear this beautiful cooking and began to long for simple sandwiches and salads prepared by myself, concluding that I could happily be a rich man for just three days.

The answer to my problems is not to buy fewer flowers, but to learn how to use a computer. I have to become independent as soon as possible. I have holidays coming up, and then two more operations. In the meanwhile I must phase the stages of my recovery so that I can overcome my fear of word processors and learn to write swiftly again. To make a good and deep recovery, I must walk lightly and maintain my sense of enchantment and elation, not keep my head buried in petty cash accounts. The happier I am, the freer I feel, the sooner I will be able to overcome the endless and banal practical problems of life, which I will do not by trying to confront them one by one, but by leaping right over them. It is realism that tells me that the only way I can solve my practical difficulties is through a magical feeling, a free spirit and a kind of intuitive intelligence as to what is appropriate.

There is a vast amount of good that will come out of bad. I will have time to write, to do research in top libraries, to meet up with excellent scholars and lawyers and political figures. The combination of the vivid experience of having lived in the frontline and the well-established facilities and institutional back-up of the North is formidable, and I must make the most of it. There are important stories to tell about the Mozambican Revolution, its triumphs and its tragedies, and then there is a huge amount of work to be done in helping to lay the foundations of the future constitution of a democratic South Africa. How many lawyers have the chance to participate both in the research leading up to the adoption of a new constitution and in the political struggles that will make its achievement possible?

Once more, I feel it is up to me; most people in my situation do not have the chances that I have, they are obliged to take advantage of every piece of assistance that comes their way. For a variety of reasons, I am privileged even as a pensionless bomb-victim amputee, even as one of the least insurable and least mortgage-worthy persons in the whole world. I have to use my imagination. This is where a certain measure of courage comes in, perhaps, not physical bravery, but courage of conception. I have something that comes to few people, a chance to reconstruct my life right from scratch. Having lost everything becomes an advantage, it opens me up to inspiration and encourages my heart to soar. No need for me to sail to Polynesia or take off on a motorbike on an anarchic journey. The bomb shattered my scheme of things and now I am free. The only crime I can commit, against myself, against my movement, against my people, is to settle for a banal and mediocre life, to accept that the big events of my existence are already over, to become a semi-retired veteran musing over the past. The biggest, most spectacular event of all, our return to a free South Africa, lies ahead. Perhaps it will not be quite as free as we dreamed of, and maybe our return will not be in conditions of total triumph as we always imagined, but basically we will have succeeded, and what a day it will be, when the ex-prisoners and detainees and exiles, the banished and the banned, are re-united in our freed homeland once more.

27

Her long wet hair drags pleasantly against my shoulder as, water splashing everywhere, she jumps out of the bath to change the record. The bathtub is not very large, and I, as the visitor on holiday from my convalescence, get the smooth part, while she as host sits less comfortably with her back to the taps, and we talk and argue and joke in the foamy water. My friend does what she wants, and right now what she wants is to hear the slow movement of the Beethoven Hammerklavier Sonata for the seventh time. I have got over my shock at detaching one movement from a piece of classical music and playing it over and over again, just as I have at her way of violating my carefully constructed daily routine of eating, sleeping and doing exercises at strict hours. I think she was alarmed when she saw me being wheeled towards her at the airport, pale and exhausted after a difficult journey, but the month is rushing by and we are having fun.

'Tell me again about the first time you went to the

occupational therapist,' she shouts laughing from the other room.

'Oh no, not again.'

'Yes, yes, you must.'

I would rather sit quietly for a few moments and think about last night, savour memories of our coming together. It was not so difficult after all, not one of those wild couplings where you pant blindly and beat and thrash and collapse exhausted afterwards, perhaps I will never have that again, perhaps I will, but a generous and loving sharing of physical intimacy between two people who had admired and felt something for each other from a distance for many years. It is not necessary to ask just what passed through her mind as she took me in her embrace, whether in her imagination she was holding the body of a hero, or of a wounded man needing love, or just of her old friend. Like me, I know she is very romantic, and also fond of finding a name for things and for joking, and that she is easily wounded, perhaps more vulnerable than I, though on the surface far more robust. I must assume that from now on and forever I will never just be me in someone's arms, but always at least in part be the wounded person, the bomb victim. Perhaps, as in everything else, it is largely up to me to create or negate the kind of universe in which I live. I am frequently amazed at the curious way love-making mixes total subjectivity and personal sentiment with extreme anonymity, so that the more profound and beautiful it is with any particular person, the more likely it is to evoke generalized memories of deep love-making with others, even leading to confusion of names and identities. Yet this time I think we were very conscious of each other, she knows she was helping me to recover confidence in my body, and we mixed in everything, fun, spontaneous occupational therapy and even intimations of real passion.

When we first sat facing each other, and our bodies had signalled their mutual openness and trust, the thought passed through my head that all men should have one of their arms chopped off, it makes us less arrogant and domineering as lovers, more equal and natural. It is not just that I had five fewer fingers to feel around with, one less arm for holding; I discovered that my whole balance was different, I lacked an elbow for leaning on and an arm to lever myself into a different position with, I was much more dependent than I had ever been on the positioning of my partner, and it was she rather than I who had to determine our mutual postures. A passage of Simone de Beauvoir came to mind, about men being all arms and legs, snatching and catching and pushing the woman's body, overwhelming her, leaving her without an inch of physical autonomy. Now I had been, not womanized, but deprived of this masculine capacity, and it left me in a state of physical uncertainty, until I began to discover that something quite lovely was happening, that it was not a choice between men reaching for women or women reaching for men, each to arouse the other and struggling more or less self-consciously to get the sequence and timing right, but that the partner could move the part of the body that he or she wished to be engaged and place it against the other's hand or mouth, taking away the waiting and sense of passivity on the one hand and the feeling of encroaching on the other. There is a generation of women who just know these things and take them for granted; how wonderful for them, and for us.

'Well . . .?' My friend leaps back into the bath with

such force that the water swirls and almost breaks over the side.

'Okay, but this is the last time,' I pretend to grumble. 'I walked through the corridors, exhausted, until I found the occupational therapy room, we call it OT. Fortunately someone had warned me that the OTs would get me to make my own tea, so when I came in, and to show how independent I was, I asked if I could make myself a cup. Just filling the kettle took ages.' I am spinning it out a bit, or, as they say here, letting the fish fry slowly.

'And then, and then?' she asks, as if she had not heard the story at least three times before, and even asked me to tell it to visitors.

'And then she wants to know what I would like to get from OT; they are very democratic, it all depends on the patient. I want my arm back, but I have to say something concrete, otherwise what will she think of me and of the ANC? So the first thing I mention is being able to look after the house. "Sweeping," I say. "Sweeping?" she queries. I think she is puzzled to find a man wanting to sweep, then I remember that no one in England sweeps anymore, at least, all the homes I know have wall-to-wall carpeting, and the owners use Hoovers and not brooms.' I know we are getting closer to the part she likes, and I shift my body in the water. 'And I want to impress her how liberated I am, so I tell her that I also want to be able to cook. "What sort of stove do you have in your house," the OT asks me, "gas or electricity?" ' My friend waits expectantly for the climax, eyes bright, lips ready for laughter. ' "I don't know", I answer.'

My friend hoots and heaves and chuckles, much as

Zuma did, and the water is in danger of swelling over the side again.

'You didn't even know if your cooker was gas or electric, and you wanted to cook.'

She has problems about being called a feminist, even a woman, says she is just a person and rebels against what she regards as the imposition of womanhood upon her, just as she rejects the subjection of men to an artificially constructed manhood. At the same time, she is highly amused at my exposure of my pretensions at being a liberated man.

'And when I was leaving the room,' I conclude the story, 'the OT calls me back and says I forgot to wash my teacup.' More laughter.

The music stops, and she rises like a porpoise surging out of the bath, her skin firm, wet and dripping, and her long hair once again trailing over my shoulder and touching my wounds. I know what she is going to ask.

'Tell me again about your first visit to the Soviet Union.' I was right, but at least I have a few more moments to myself. I like the little interludes to our joking sessions in the bath, the moments of quiet when I can luxuriate passively in the afterglow of intimacy.

Intimacy. This is the only area where I am really worried. Physically I am going to be okay, I can handle the question of image without too much difficulty, even the thing of being called a hero, and the money and professional side will work themselves out. The big problem is love. This is not just my problem, it is everybody's. I feel an openness such as I have never had, an almost reckless disregard of consequences and willingness to fly that I have always admired in others but never possessed myself. Faintly, faintly in the background,

I have an inkling of distrust of the brilliant and free physical emotion and hints of a fear that it will burn and consume whatever it touches, but right now I am enjoying myself too much to want to rein in. My friend is courageous and strong, she takes me everywhere, to the beach, to the theatre, to the best ice-cream shop in town, gets me to read aloud for hours after midnight because she loves to hear my voice speaking English, introduces me to writers and musicologists and politicians, supervises my exercises, holds my hand as I enter the water, finds a new restaurant each day. She explains to me what post-modernism is, and shows me a cluster of recent post-modernist constructions, and when I ask her what has happened in the European music world in the last decade, she tells me about the opera *Lulu* and then interrupts her playing of the Hammerklavier slow movement to put the macabre and beautiful music on the record-player instead. We splash and speak wittily to each other in the bath, enjoy our food and from time to time spend our nights in the same bed. It took me years and years to learn to share a bed with another, but now I feel I sleep better with a breathing body at my side and the security of knowing that each night there will be a farewell embrace and hug and each morning we can roll and curl up against each other. I have to be a little more attentive to how I place my pillows, and careful not to allow too much pressure on my wounds, but otherwise the bed-sharing is proving easy, and I feel relieved and glad that one of the biggest physical and emotional advances I have made in my post-bomb life has been in the company of an intellectual.

'Well?' she asks, settling back into the water.

'Let's run some more hot water,' I urge, 'then I'll tell you.'

We add hot water and a few drops of bubble-bath to renew the foam, which now nearly spills over. I love leaning my legs against hers as we talk, the foam covering them like a blanket.

'It was 1954,' I say. 'Stalin had been dead a year, and we were the first group from the West about to travel on a slow train to China. I was very young. Imagine our excitement. I had a friend, Wolfie, in Cape Town who always had a good collection of magazines, in two distinct piles, one from the Soviet Union and China, with titles like *Soviet Women* and *China Reconstructs*, the other from the USA, like *Time* and *Life*, which he got, he explained, because you had to know what the enemy was thinking. So we always went to Wolfie's and made a dive to read what the enemy was thinking, we did not have money to buy our own copies, and then we glanced dutifully at the literature from the socialist countries. Certain images stuck in my mind, mainly of co-operative farm workers, dressed in white in front of tables weighed down by food, with rows and rows of combine-harvesters in the background. Now the train was about to carry me and a few hundred others from Prague to Moscow and then on to Peking.

'After a slow journey through Czechoslovakia, the train began to approach the Soviet border. My heart was going boom-boom-boom, we were about to enter the first socialist state. In the fields I could see Slovak women dressed in black with dark headscarves harvesting crops with sickles. Wait till we cross the border, I said to myself, then we will see the difference. The train arrived at the border, and after due formalities, chugged across. We were in the Soviet Union, and there in the fields were women dressed in black with dark headscarves reaping crops with sickles. Well, I said

154

to myself, this is the part annexed only after the Second World War, wait till we get to the older section. The next day, deep in the interior, I could see women dressed in black with headscarves reaping with sickles. Okay, this was the part occupied by the Nazis, wait till we get to the other part, and of course when we got there, there too were women dressed in black, et cetera.

'That was a huge disappointment, but it was difficult to say so, I thought there was something wrong with me, not the reality I was seeing. Then about twenty-five years later I went again . . . you want to hear about all my trips?'

'Yes.'

'. . . and Moscow looked amazingly green and spacious, the greenest city I had ever seen, and we were taken up to the Lomonosov University up on the hill, there's a pre-post-modernist building for you, Stalin-style, and as we were looking at the city I recalled having been on that spot before and hearing the guide say I should come back twenty years later, there would be a sports stadium here and a housing development for one million people on this side and half a million on the other, and there I was seeing it all exactly as the guide had said, and once more the Soviet Union had taken me by surprise.

'Then a few years later I went again on my way back from a journey to India. It was just after Ruth First was killed, and I was feeling terrible, in fact I had mononucleosis without knowing it, and decided I would rather be sick in England than anywhere else. Getting an earlier plane from Moscow proved to be extremely difficult, and the person looking after me suggested that I offer one of the scarves I had brought from India to the booking clerk as it was her Saint's

Day. He took the scarf, and I got my seat and felt even more sick, the plane was almost empty.

'Last year three of us went as "ANC social scientists" to meet academics in the Soviet Union, and once more I was astonished, this time by the openness and vivacity of the discussion, surely the world's most exciting intellectual centre at that moment. We even had to try to persuade them that some of their policies had been right. The atmosphere was amazing, wonderful. Okay, enough?'

'Enough.'

It is not everybody who discusses perestroika in the bath. We also plan the menu for her birthday party, and like all her countrymen and women, she gets excited just by talking about food. The water is pleasantly warm, the bubbles are popping softly, she washes my back and lets the spray run on the spots that give me most delight. I could happily spend the rest of the month just sitting in the bath with her, feeling the unconstrained vitality of her wit, leaning my legs against hers.

'Time to get out,' she says. She enjoys taking command, treating me in a humorous and affectionate way as a slightly slow schoolboy. She springs up, water tumbling down her breasts, and leaps out of the bath. The Beethoven slow movement has reached moments of quietly ecstatic beauty. My body is tingling, my heart is lighter than it has been for months. I exult, therefore I am.

Leaning my left forearm against the side of the bath I try to raise myself but plunge unceremoniously back in again. I struggle to turn myself around, but now there is nowhere to put my arm. I wriggle my body back into its initial position, and try to lift my backside again. Slowly, slowly, I tell myself, take a breath, get well into position, and up. I push with all my force and lift and lift . . . yes, I've made it, my bottom is on the side of the bath. But now I have to lift my legs over, and I am scared I will fall back into the bath and break a limb, how humiliating. Slowly, slowly, I lift my one leg until it is resting on the edge and slowly and slowly, lower it on the other side. I am perched most uncomfortably, my bum is hurting, and I cannot move either forward or back. Slowly, slowly, I begin to raise the other leg, slowly, slowly and over it goes. Viva, hooray.

I stand up, laughing at the ludicrous exit from the bath, and suddenly find myself shouting and cursing. 'You bloody bastards who did this to me,' rage is bursting out for the first time, but as I say these words to myself I remember my friend who said he was born outside of marriage and did not like the word 'bastard,' 'You bloody buggers who blew off my arm,' and then I recall that the word 'bugger' could be regarded as anti-homosexual, 'you bloody shits who planted the bomb and tried to kill me, we'll get you one day, don't think you will escape, you bloody rats, you cockroaches, you scum,' primitive anger surging up and released not by bitterness but by sudden and deep joy.

28

Perched up on the stage and looking at the audience filing in and taking their seats, I have difficulty believing that this major hall in one of the world's greatest universities can be so shabby. Everything looks old and discoloured; if it had been a cinema, it would have been converted long ago, but it seems intellectuals in England feel at home with discomfort. Perhaps it is one of the effects of the government cuts in university budgets, but right now I am feeling tense and irritable and want somebody to blame. Why is the Left so style-less? There was no one to fetch me, no one waiting to receive me when I arrived, there is no cloth on the table, no flowers, there will not be any songs or music, everyone, myself included, will speak in low, flat tones, there will be no emotion, no atmosphere, no fun, no sparkle. The fact is that I am not only sluggish and heavy after my second operation, I have a severe illness which the doctors have failed completely to diagnose, namely, meeting-phobia. I am sure that it started pre-natally, when the only exercises my mother did were running off leaflets and standing in a picket line.

Someone should explain to me why rock concerts should have so much vivacity and our gatherings be so drab. I watched the Nelson Mandela concert for hours on TV – in part, it is true, I was trying to see my children in the crowd – and not just from excitement at viewing 70,000 young British people supporting our struggle and having fun at the same time; the visual spectacle was always interesting and there was lots of humour and emotion. In the background of one of the stages was a huge blow-up of a painting by Malangatana, one of my many close friends from the artistic community in Mozambique. At even the tiniest meeting in Maputo there would be a cloth on the table and a jam tin with a pot-plant, not to speak of songs, even Parliament resounded frequently with songs. Imagine the Queen or Mrs Thatcher opening a session of Westminster with a song.

My first post-bomb meeting, like my first shoelace or

my first chopped onion, was an important occasion for me. It was at the headquarters of Amnesty International; I came straight from the physio gym, thinking hard in the minicab about what I was going to say. Amnesty were about to send a delegation to Mozambique to check up on reports it had received of violations of human rights in that country, and they wanted to hear from me before they went. All those faces staring at me, a heavy atmosphere in the room, I was deeply anxious, not just because the session was being recorded on tape and film and I might say something unguarded or offensive, but because until then all my thinking and talking had been about me, and now the subject was something other than myself, and I was not sure if my jealous self-centredness would allow me to speak properly. On occasions in hospital when comrades visiting me had started discussing the world scene, I had found myself grabbing the conversation and forcing it back to describing how my ankle was getting on. I felt ashamed, but could not control myself.

At Amnesty I spoke about Mozambique, but in terms of my own experience as a lawyer working and living there, how I felt at the different stages, the elation of the early years when we were building up a system of courts from scratch, the shock later on when a whipping law was introduced to deal with black-marketeering, the struggle in an underdeveloped country to materialize things with virtually no means – you can never isolate an issue, the problems have problems behind them, we could not print legislation because of shortage of paper, or there would be electricity cuts or the petrol would run out, or we would wait months for an overworked Minister to take a decision on some tiny issue.

All the time as I was speaking the question was

running around in my mind: did the rich and the poor have the same human rights problems? In Mozambique we were fighting against hunger, to eliminate diseases like measles that killed thousands of kids every year, for schools, for elementary knowledge, to be a nation with a distinct personality and not, as the colonialists would have had it, a collection of tribes, of natives, existing on the periphery of or even right outside history and politics. And now the war was engulfing everything, destroying clinics and schools and courts, and devastating the national psyche. The idea of solving all problems by running to your lawyer was just ludicrous, we had less than a hundred lawyers for a population of millions. The smugness of the West angered me, the assumption that it had human rights in such abundance that it had a surplus for export.

Yet one could not run away from the due process issue, the right to a fair trial, the repudiation of torture and locking people up for ever without bringing them to court. We could point to all the problems of underdevelopment left behind by colonialism, the tragedies inflicted on the country by South African destabilization, but they did not excuse or justify a single act of violence against prisoners or keeping people in detention for months, even years, just because some official was unwilling to make a decision. More and more it seemed clear to me that there were now certain values and procedures that belonged not to the West but to all humanity. They had been fought for over the centuries in many countries and many continents, usually by the 'loony Left' of the time, and frequently established only after the use of armed struggle and much sacrifice, and today they were the patrimony of all peoples, independently of their geographical location

160

or political systems or religious or cultural beliefs. After decades of arguing for and believing in a law-in-context perspective, and after devoting most of my talk to doing just that in relation to Mozambique, I was surprised at the vehemence with which I pleaded for universal values.

The next talk was at Oxford; billed as a seminar at the Refugees Studies Centre; the small room was packed, and I stood so as to be able to see everybody. Once again, I was rigid with tension, I felt I still had to regain my capacity for looking at and speaking to so many people at a time. There was a strong atmosphere of sadness and anxiety in the room, people had come to see as much as to hear me. We showed the film on art and the war, and the atmosphere became softer. I argued that refugees should have human rights that went beyond the right not to be repatriated against their will and the right to food and shelter, fundamental though they were – they should have the right to choose their own representatives, to participate in the administration of programmes and to complain about abusive behaviour towards them. These rights should be built up steadily over the years, just as poor relief was progressively transformed from a system of benevolence to one of welfare rights in Britain. I also suggested that as far as possible refugees should be seen not simply as a drain on the host society but as contributors towards cultural enrichment and as economic producers, and that instead of aid agencies elaborating relief programmes for persons autonomized in camps, there be regional development planning that integrated rather than segregated the camp population. Although I spoke as someone from Mozambique with its vast refugee population, almost everything I said was based on reading I had done at Oxford, and I did not feel I was speaking with real authority.

The question and answer session went well, I even managed a few smiles, and then I felt my thigh weakening. It was as though it was sending a message up to my brain: tell the tongue to end now, it is talking too much and I'm getting tired. The tongue answered (all this while I am dealing with the question of the complexes that people from rich countries have when dealing with those from poor lands): tell the thigh that the timing will be just right, I know when to stop. The timing was exactly right, the session ended warmly, I was happy that I had established rapport with the audience, and I started to sit down. The muscles in my leg locked tight, and I could not bend my knee. It was too late to prevent the plunge, my body was too far down in its descent, and I felt myself tumbling towards the floor. As I crashed down, my leg twisted and bounced, and pain mixed with my bewilderment and ignominy. The audience gasped out loud, people rushed forward. 'Stay away, stay away!' I shouted, with the pride and anger of a disabled person cross with himself. I managed to struggle up off the floor but felt sick and humilated for hours afterwards, and I could not even blame it on Oxford.

At Warwick University, where I went next, I remained firmly in my seat. According to the daughter of some old friends of mine with whom I had been staying, the students at Cambridge (her university) regarded me like Che Guevara: they knew I had done something though they did not know quite what. At Warwick I sensed there was more knowledge and less adulation. The auditorium was packed, the questions were extensive but friendly, and I did not topple.

The hardest engagement of all was at Southampton University, where, as I told them, during six years of teaching I had got to know England. I needed to be rested before undergoing emotional experiences, to be strong and serene so as to break the sadness of those who see me without an arm, and I was tired when I arrived. There were all my former Law Faculty colleagues in one room, anxious like any talk organizers about whether I would arrive on time. I smiled, and shook their hands and received a few hugs, but I was exhausted, it was only days after I had come out of hospital and I just could not break the heaviness. The talk I gave dealt in an intimate and personal way with the whole experience of the bomb and the process of recovery. Half-way through I felt faint, my head was light and I thought I might fall over. I asked for a short interval, drank some water, and then continued. It was a good meeting, at times I managed some light humour, and felt the beginnings of my capacity to talk easily and freely coming back (when I cannot give an impromptu talk on almost any subject, I know I am dead), but sensed that I was still a long way from being able to engage normally with the public and break out of my total preoccupation with myself.

I look down at the audience. The shabby auditorium is almost full, people are quiet as they look up at me. The chairperson is a distinguished solicitor who over the decades opened his home to freedom fighters from all over Africa. I once accompanied him as interpreter in Mozambique, and remember with amusement how at a meeting one night under moonlit palm trees in the beautiful Island of Mozambique, I had to interpret the question: how was the armed struggle of the people of England going?

The chairperson pushes his seat back – how ugly it is – and I tense myself for giving my first talk in Britain on the subject which from a political point of view has most occupied my mind these past few years, and which, I hinted to the *New York Times*, could have led to the attack on my life ('every intellectual likes to be taken seriously').

How marvellous it would be if he started the meeting off with a song, and the audience joined in with four-part harmony, if guitars and flutes started playing, if beautifully painted banners with lots of colour and no slogans suddenly appeared, and a jam tin with a little plant in it was put on the table.

'Ladies and gentlemen, friends and comrades,' he is speaking good no-nonsense English prose in low and precise tones, 'it gives me great pleasure to see you all here in this hall in the London School of Economics and Political Science on the occasion of the annual D.N. Pritt Memorial Lecture, which tonight will be given by Albie Sachs. The subject he has chosen is: "Towards a Bill of Rights in a Democratic South Africa".'

29

All revolutions are impossible until they happen, then they become inevitable. South Africa is trembling between the impossible and the inevitable . . . No, that is how I started my pamphlet, I cannot quote myself all the time.

South Africa must be unique in the world as the only country where sections of the oppressed have set up an anti-Bill of Rights Committee . . . Yes, after saying a few words about what Pritt, the English barrister who defended

African patriots, meant to us in South Africa, I will plunge in with these opening words. There is always a thrilling and frightening moment when I stand up and decide exactly how I am going to launch my talk. Once when walking a few paces to a lectern I felt overwhelming fatigue at the talk I had planned to give, and as I stepped to the microphone, I launched into an entirely different topic, and it came off wonderfully well. Ever since then I have half feared and half hoped that I will find myself risking yet another sudden *salto mortal*, a leap into nothingness. Not tonight, I have to shepherd my emotional resources carefully; in part it is I, the speaker, who is the message, I must show that, like the ANC and our people's struggle, I have not been destroyed.

. . . *their fear was that a Bill of Rights would simply be a means of entrenching white privilege.* It is strange hearing my voice. I am still learning to speak again, to project my words to all those faces staring rather grimly at me. Every syllable has to be forced out, it is like rediscovering my bowel control, it does not just come naturally, my will has to direct each detail. When I used to talk, before, I just stood up and the words came through spontaneously, it was fun, I became animated. Now it is exhausting, a deliberate labour. I have to think through the sounds, the sense, the emotion, work out every statement in advance, say it to my inner mind before forcing it out to the audience. *Take land ownership: 87 per cent of the land by law belongs to the whites, and probably 95 per cent of the country's productive capacity. A simple property clause in a Bill of Rights could freeze this situation of de facto apartheid forever. What sort of human rights protection would it be if the millions of victims of forced removals, bulldozed in recent years out of their ancestral lands*

*by apartheid officials, had to bow before the constitutionally
protected titles of the new owners . . .?*

Why do we use such heavy formulations when we
talk in public, why do we not just chat away? That
strained voice I can hear, it is mine; if I am not self-
conscious about speaking, I am about hearing. I am
listening to myself even as I prepare the next phrase
. . . *Yet we need a Bill of Rights. Too often in the name
of the Revolution, of social progress, of development and
nation-building, basic human rights have been ignored. We
want our people, all our people, to be able to sleep freely in
their homes at night, to walk freely in the streets, to feel that
the country, the whole country, belongs to them all, that the
government is answerable to and changeable by them . . .*

It is going easily now, I have given this presentation
many times, the most important one being at our own
ANC in-house seminar (revolutionaries are getting chic
these days) shortly before the bomb, and the interesting thing is that I do not feel I have to change
a word depending on who the audience is, whether
freedom fighters in Africa, lawyers in England, or
business people in New York. We have simple justice
on our side, it is a question of finding the right way to
formulate our claims. It is not just a matter of getting
rid of overtly racist laws; the whole system of de facto
apartheid, the accumulated injustice of centuries of racial
domination and inequality has to be replaced, as rapidly
and as painlessly as possible. This is the hardest part
in speaking to a Western audience, they just cannot
understand our psychology or goals. We speak the same
political language as they do, have the same concepts of
what is right and wrong, but we are not politicians such
as they know, we are not running for office, we are
freedom fighters who are fearful of rather than spurred

on by the thought of office. Nor for our friends on the Left are we always comfortable with the notion of infinitely postponable goals, of working out some kind of ideal society that we would like to live in at some indefinite date. We are part of a historic freedom movement, very concrete, rooted in our history and culture, many of our forebears struggled with spear in hand to defend their lands, others later preached in churches and mosques, organized trade unions, always with the single dream of a South Africa without racial domination. Mandela's years in prison, Ruth's death, the trauma of the thousands and thousands of detainees, all those tortured to death, it must mean something, it was not just for a few people to get into office. We are not strong enough right now to rise up and overthrow the racist regime, nor are they able to crush us. We might find ourselves confronted with hard decisions, whether to hold out for generations if necessary, until we are finally able to overthrow and completely destroy the system of apartheid, or to accept major but incomplete breakthroughs now, transforming the terrain of struggle in a way which is advantageous to the achievement of our ultimate goals. In the end we have to find a way of consulting with the people to find out what they feel, and this means struggling for the opening of the jails and the return of the exiles and the creation of conditions of free discussion and consultation.

Our constitutional guidelines are already circulating inside the country. They are not cut-and-dried, but open to enrichment and amendment, in big things and in small.

Finding the moment to end is always difficult. I am usually so eager to finish on a high note that I talk on and on, and so make the task even more complicated. Yet this would be a good moment to stop, inviting the audience not just as a courtesy but as a political contribution to offer their criticisms and suggestions.

And this is where we look to our friends abroad as well. Help us with your criticism, force us to argue and think through our proposals. The greatest solidarity you can offer is to take our proposals seriously and subject them to critical and sceptical analysis . . . The floor is open.

The applause is strong, and I look round at the people clapping. There are very few faces that I recognize, I think there are others of my generation who are meeting-tired. The audience is like the people you would see outside on the streets, there are young and old, people in smart city suits and others in jeans and pullovers, black and white, about half men, half women. Their faces are animated, they are buzzing a little, and the auditorium somehow looks less bare.

The chairperson stands up and offers as his sceptical bit the advice given by the rebels in the fifteenth-century revolt of the men of Kent: hang all the lawyers. The discussion is thrown open to the floor.

The questions flow rapidly, the nondescript, anonymous audience crystallizes into distinct personalities, speaking with humour and vivacity. There is strong feeling on the subject, well-informed questioning. This is the English intellectual way, no fuss, no show-off, let the words and the ideas come through cleanly and simply. In a world dominated by consumerism and advertising, by show business and PR, it requires conscious determination not to be sucked into the business of image-making and reducing ideas to packaged products, that is the other message of this meeting that I have to take with me. Some of those present turn out to be students from the University of Cape Town, where I qualified all those years ago, and they are excited by the themes, and want me to participate in a phone-in debate in the Law Faculty . . . Other suggestions come through about how we can get discussion going on our ideas. I would not say the hall looks attractive, but the chairs are definitely not quite as ugly as they were, and the stage not quite so bare, though I would give up my drink at the pub afterwards (in this case, my meal with the committee) for some flowers, assuming that pot-plants in jam tins are not available here.

30

I had a dream . . . The other night some people came round and we were chatting about this and that when I interrupted the conversation to mention a thought that had just popped into my head.

'I wonder,' I said, 'when I have a dream and I appear in my dream, if I have two arms or only one.'

The visitors were a little taken aback by this statement, which to me appeared to be quite ordinary. It was a question of scientific curiosity more than anything else: I really wanted to know if my unconscious had come to terms with my physical reality or not, and if not, how long the lag would be.

Last night, or rather, early this morning, just as I was about to wake up, my unconscious answered me. At first I was not aware that I was dreaming, I just had an awareness of a close physical presence, something carnal and attractive and warm at my side, almost touching me. Then I made out that it was a woman's body, sitting upright, round and plump and clad in attractive blue material so that I could not see any flesh. I looked upward to identify the person, and noted that there was a woman's face; in fact, the features changed while I was looking at them, first of an older person whom I recognized with some surprise, and then of a younger one, something like my friend with whom I had holidayed. She was smiling and quite friendly, and I sat at her side and put my right arm around her. My arm was long and reached right past her shoulder to the front of her. I was aware of my hand under the fabric of the blue dress, curving round her ribs and reaching to her breast. I stayed in that position for quite a while, feeling aroused in a warm and comfortable way. Then for some reason that was not clear to me I disengaged my arm, pulled it out from under her dress and curled it back across her shoulder. We were separated and I felt a bit strange, as though a lot had taken place and yet nothing had happened.

Now, having just woken, I am thinking about my dream, and trying to work it out. The images are still clear in my mind, and I have a slightly unsettled sensation coupled with a rather warm afterglow. I can work out who the faces represented, two women both on the plump side, both fair-haired, both cheerful, whom I knew in totally different contexts; with one I had been physically involved, while with the other I had been in close proximity and maybe we had both thought about it, but it had been impossible. The conjugation of the two is surprising, the way the small wrinkles of the one gave way to the smooth features of the other, but there is a kind of logic in the shapes and personalities of the two tied in with my general feelings about heavier women, but that is not the really interesting part.

The bit of the dream that stands out, like a twist at the end of an O. Henry short story, relates to what was passing through my mind as I withdrew my arm. I have a distinct recollection of saying to myself while still dreaming: you know, that was strange, my arm was there, it was under the dress, but I could feel nothing . . . I wanted to feel her breast and experience the intense tactile intimacy, but I took away no sensation at all, neither of her breast nor of the flesh around her shoulder, because I had no fingers.

I am not sure why, but this answer from my unconscious pleases me. I somehow feel that the more my unconscious gets to grips with my reality – the inverse of the usual psychoanalytical goal – the quicker my full recovery will be.

31

Her fingertips cascade ceaselessly and exquisitely down my back.

'You mean to say you had to come to Vienna to have your first massage?'

'Yes.'

'But London has wonderful massage.'

'I never believed in it, thought it was too self-indulgent.'

'You can never be too kind to your body.'

Each rippling stroke of her fingers seems to be dissolving the last remaining links in the chain-mail of my bodily puritanism. I could accept friendly hands if they made me better or stronger or were part of a game or erotic activity, but stroking just for the sake of pleasure was an indulgence of the idle rich who had no better way to spend their time. Now the gentle and rhythmic tickling down my shoulders and spine are inducing serenity and delight in my whole body, and making me intensely glad that I accepted the offer to spend some time in Vienna with Margit and other friends like this former colleague of mine. Her movements are emotionally healing, but above all they are pleasurable in themselves, and I must just relax on my stomach in the cool, dark room, and enjoy it.

In Maputo, where some years back we were both working as legal advisers, I had been the confident, dominating one in conversation. We would be talking about war and destabilization and revolution and counter-revolution, and she would find a moment to argue that feet were more important than hands as determinants of personality.

'Do you still believe that your personality is based on your foot?' I ask.

'Yes. The nerve-endings in your feet reach into all parts of your body, and the relationship between your feet and the rest of your body indicates what kind of person you are.' She is as eager to explain her concepts as we used to be about the labour theory of value or the role of the white working class in the South African struggle.

Perhaps we are just conjunctions of muscle and bone and skin and body fluids, and all the rest, the mental constructs and all the striving, the goals, the dreams and suffering, is merely illusion. I had a friend in Harare whose belief in bath oil therapy was as strong as mine in the inevitability of armed struggle as a component part of the freedom process in Southern Africa. Maybe this is the moment to give up all the endless combat, the debate over ideas, the attempts to better the world, and relax once and for ever into the mysteries and secret interdependencies of the body. At least one's body is a whole entity, not fragmented into a million egos and currents and contradictory trends like political movements.

The delicate finger-tracings cover my right shoulder and proceed fluently and lovingly down my traumatized short arm. I tremble quietly inside, intensely moved by the kindness and the sensual consolation established in my zone of damage.

'You are lucky it was your right arm that was affected.' She is speaking with quiet force, and I wonder if she has made a mistake with her English.

'But I used to be right-handed, or rather, I was ambidextrous.' I never miss a chance to make the joke. 'I was equally useless with both hands.'

'That's what I mean, our right arms are aggressive, especially with men, we keep the world away with our right hands, we try to dominate everything with them, while our left arms express the gentle and receiving sides of our natures. Now you will have to use the kinder side of yourself in dealing with the world, and you will come out a more balanced person. You can make a gentle arm more active, but it is very difficult to make a dominant arm more gentle.'

She has never spoken to me with such certainty. Just as my experience in solitary confinement all those years ago made me intensely aware of my psyche, so the blast has put me actively and at times overwhelmingly in touch with my body. Yesterday Margit and I and my friend and her companion all went to the municipal hot springs and sauna. It was the evening for nude bathing and the four of us wandered around with the quiet intimacy and unconstrained friendliness that nudity brings. I valued very much the accepting comrade-ship of the hundreds of other nude bathers, people of Vienna who knew nothing about me, but shared a spontaneous nakedness and made me feel welcome as I am in their ranks.

'You know something?' she continues with a soft, serious voice, while her fingers caress my shoulder-blade at the point where all the nerves from my arm seemed to meet. 'I could only give you this massage today because you were willing to receive it. We have to learn to receive as well as to give. Most of us don't know how to receive.'

I find it easier to accept massage as a sensual rather than an existential experience, but I can feel that there is something different in our relationship, a plastic sense of giving and taking. Her body and hand movements are rhythmical and intensely personal to me. There is no erotic commitment, but a strong sense of mutual body relationship, and a very personalized form of giving, an intimate, and what she would regard as a feminist world-view being expressed, and I am learning to receive it. This question of gender-related world-views and modes of self-affirmation worries me. The other night I gave a little talk at Margit's place about the bomb experience and as I got to the part where I wished to mention how much I appreciated visits from women friends at the hospital because men did not know how to express physical affection and tenderness, I noticed with a sense of panic that Margit's and my gay rights friend was in the audience. At one time in my life I would have rejected any idea of gender-associated differences, especially if they were used in any way to justify privilege and exclusion, but now I feel that we men, freedom fighters not excluded, are definitely lacking in capacity to express important human qualities and that the world as a whole could benefit from being a little more feminized, or, rather, de-masculinized. The problem was what our friend would think: the idea of male-female or female-female tenderness was easy for me to accept; more difficult was the notion of male-male tenderness, not for any reasons of principle but because of habit. Then I had a bit of luck. Just as I got to the crucial part, his eyes closed and he fell asleep.

'Did you enjoy the sauna yesterday?' She knows the answer to her question, but wants to revive pleasant memories.

'I need a stronger word than "enjoy", and much as I loved the sauna the big thing was going in the pools.'

My attempts earlier to swim in England were fraught with misery. Stephanie took me one afternoon to the house of a physiotherapist friend who happened to be deeply religious ('I prayed for Albie, I hope he doesn't mind' – I did not mind, I was thrilled) and who had a large, heated swimming pool. I had not seen Stephanie in a bathing costume for over ten years, our last holiday together at the beach had been painful for us both, and now we were like a couple visiting our friends again, and Stephanie was holding my body as I slipped uncomfortably into the water. Our kisses and hugs in the hospital had been very correct, we spoke about our lives, the children, the struggle, but we had not had contact flesh against flesh as in the swimming pool. The water terrified me. My body was chilled, I felt myself slipping all the time, unable to adjust to the slightest flow or current. Stephanie and her friend supported me as I tried to float on my back. I was desperate and could not wait to leave the pool, much as I appreciated the solidarity and love I was receiving.

Last night, in between sitting in really hot saunas during which experts at towel-waving caused the steamy hot air to whip and circulate across our sweating shoulders, I plunged happily into icy troughs and then into the hot spring pools. The water jetted and bubbled everywhere, and, encouraged by the sense of naturalness which nudity gave us, I found myself moving further and further from the protection of my group. Holding on to the side of the pool I pranced this way and that, my sense of happiness increasing as I discovered renewed freedom to pull my body through the water. At a certain moment I found myself next to a rubber flap that I knew served as the gateway to an outdoor pool. Yes, yes, I said to myself, I'm going outside. The stars were faintly visible in the dark night sky, and steam rose from the water into the chill air. I was almost alone outside, dim shadowy structures surrounded the pool. Yes, yes, I repeated, I can do it. I moved to a corner and launched my body into the water, ready to swallow and choke if necessary. Frantically I moved my left arm forward and executed a series of dog-paddles, managing to kick my legs at the same time. One stroke, two, three, four, five . . . I was across the corner and holding joyously on to the other side of the pool. Five strokes, and I had kept my head above the water, and breathed, and felt exactly the same sensation of triumph I had had when, aged six, I had done five strokes and kept my head up and breathed at the Johannesburg Zoo Lake swimming baths.

'I learnt to swim again, it was wonderful.'

The delicate touching is now going like a slow, warm wave across my back, a lovely provocation that reaches down and down, further and further . . . and stops. I am lying entranced and tingling, aware that there are still areas of my body that have not been touched. My friend adjusts her posture, and begins to put oil on my legs. I am not so sure about this . . . oil on me? . . . it makes my skin and muscles feel good, but reminds me of the idle rich, of Cleopatra rather than her slaves. The tickling arousal starts at my feet and moves slowly upwards, across my ankles that always get stiff and painful when I walk, along the calf, behind and over my knee, on to my thigh, passing the zones that still have shrapnel, up and up, where my skin is specially sensitive, further and further . . . and stops.

My whole body is in a state of pleasant arousal, the room is quiet, and I do not wish the massage ever to end. I am going to give up the freedom struggle, and I am going to lie on this bed forever, in a condition of permanent giving–and–receiving bliss.

'You are lucky that you are going back to London,' my friend tells me.

'Why?'

'Because you have the best massage centres in the world there. There are many different kinds of massage, many different techniques and theories. Some believe in massaging internal organs, others in massaging muscles, others concentrate on body fluids. Massaging your muscles might even be harmful, you have to be careful not to go to the wrong kind of massagists, it is much better to work with body fluids, and there is this centre in London, the Bio . . .'

Oh no, in the midst of my bodily bliss my soul is groaning, oh no, they have more ideological splits than we do, so it is back to the freedom struggle . . . but not quite yet, o Lord, just one more cascade of her fingers along my bodily fluids, and then I will return.

32

I wanted to be mothered by everyone in the whole world, except by my mother. There she sits across the stage, Stephanie and the children at her side, some black in her hair despite her eighty-four years, as she proudly points out. It is theatre in the round, so we can all see each other as well as the stage, and the Young Vic is packed, with people unable to get in. They have come to see a special benefit performance of *The Jail Diary of Albie Sachs* and they know from all the media publicity that I am in the audience, and will be called on to say a few words at the end.

When I was about nine and my mother wanted to hold my hand as we crossed the road, I pushed her fingers away and crossed on my own. I was a little amazed at my action, but in fact, though we have been quite affectionate over the years, I have never taken her hand back in mine. Only when I feel strong and adult am I able to accept her mothering. I am sure she is proud to be sitting with her grandchildren and former daughter-in-law, about to see for the first time a play about her son. When she arrived in London it was hard for us both; if one of my sons ever came to me with a missing limb, however I might appear on the outside, I would be weeping inside. I was not strong enough to be weak with her. We spent a strenuous week-end together, she, two of her sisters and myself, smiling all the time. One of my aunts, who used to knit me jerseys as a child, always shakes her head at me, saying that with my brains and all the scholarships I got, I could have been really successful, become a judge. I have an old schoolfriend from Cape Town who did in fact become a judge, he is even a Sir here in England, and when we recently spent a weekend together at his family cottage in the Cotswolds we acknowledged without declaration that we were both happy with our lives; he had wanted to be a judge and became a judge and I had wanted to be a freedom fighter and became a freedom fighter.

My mother is talking animatedly to Stephanie; she reminisces a lot, has discovered that there is great interest in the past. I wonder if she is telling the story about how she and Josie Mpama were sent to organize the mineworkers in their compounds, it was easier for women to get through, and it was winter and freezing cold and they only had one pair of gloves between them, so that they would take it in turns, first she would wear the left glove and Josie the right, then the other way round.

David Edgar, who made the play out of my book, says that on the day after the explosion, four Albie Sachses got in touch with him to find out how I was getting on, and goes on to explain that they were all actors who had played the part in various productions. Now all of them are appearing in this special performance, one playing me again, the others playing various policemen. I have seen the play once; I was passing through London and managed to catch a revival of the original production by the Royal Shakespeare Company. There was an American tourist sitting next to me, and during the interval I felt several times like nudging him and saying: you know something . . .?, but for reasons of dignity, Mozambican-style, did not do so. At first I was astonished at the interest in the play, the full houses, a special ticket had to be found

179

for me; nothing happened, in fact it was a play about nothing happening, no interactional drama, no deep philosophical or existential insights, just a quiet series of variations based on the details of my thoughts and emotions while in solitary confinement. Then it occurred to me that perhaps this was exactly what gave the story its interest, the fact that the central figure was so ordinary and quiet that each spectator could identify with him and wonder how he or she would have reacted in similar circumstances.

Tonight the theatricality will be intensified. The audience will wonder as they see the person representing me how I am identifying with him, and will also be trying to imagine how the actor feels knowing that I am watching him playing me. In fact it is even more complicated, because I know that he will be wondering how I feel about his representation of me, and he knows that I know, and we both know that the audience will be wondering about how we feel about knowing that we each know about the other knowing . . . and so on and so on. If we fail tonight, we should all give up theatre. My problem is what to say afterwards, how I can make my contribution in a way that will intensify the emotion of the evening rather than banal–ize it.

I would like to greet my mother. She would never take the initiative in waving to me here, she remembers how I used to hate her even attending school prize-givings. I wait till I can catch her attention, and then wave strongly towards her, and gesture to indicate that I want to wave to the children as well. A few people are looking without looking in my direction.

The play is about to begin, there is some African music in the background, the actor walks quietly on to the stage, and we are no longer just people sitting in a

180

theatre but spectators at a play. I am going to enjoy the performance. I have forgotten everything, the original experience, the book, the play, I am just a spectator, ready to laugh and be moved. That is one of the great things about writing it all out; when the book is ready, and after those sensual and thrilling moments when you run your fingers through the pages of the first copies, the experience is eliminated and you can get on with your life. What I like about the present situation is the idea that the young Albie, struggling with the fires of his inner anguish and winning through, but only just, is coming to the aid of the middle-aged Albie. David did a fine job converting what is really a prolonged interior monologue into a piece of theatre.

'So this is what it's like . . .' The actor is describing the cell and what it is like to be locked up in a concrete cube. I look at his hair, listen to his voice, the slight South African accent, and make myself open to what he is projecting. The audience is laughing at the little jokes and bits of irony, you can feel their involvement increasing as the story slowly presents itself, there is a strong sense of intimacy, of closeness of endeavour, of willingness to share a series of mirrored experiences. I am glad the person down there on the stage is coming through well, that the audience seems to like him, and think what he has to say interesting. The whistling moment catches me off guard, the beautiful strains of the 'Going Home' theme from Dvořák's New World Symphony, which I whistled to some unknown person in the prison who whistled them back to me; I feel tears start whenever I hear it. The first act is nearly over, and the actor is talking about how one day he will write a play, set in a prison . . . I remember how passionately in jail I hugged to myself the idea of the play. It was my way of fighting my isolation, of wrestling with the sense of being something worthless and without significance in the world. Constructing the play in my mind was an imaginative activity that gave me personality at that moment and also promised me a future audience that would be listening to this person, helping him break out of solitary confinement, believing in him, admiring him, even applauding. On my happiest days, or, rather, during my least depressed moments, I even fantasized that the play would be put on in a London theatre, somehow the thought of English applause was worth double the applause anywhere else. Now I am in a London theatre, and I will be joining in the clapping.

'. . . and the hardest thing will be to convey to the audience exactly what it is like to be locked up alone, with nothing to do except stare at the wall and your feet . . . I will ask the audience just to stare for three minutes at the stage where nothing happens . . . just three minutes . . .' David put this skilfully at the end of act one, and the actor is sitting down quietly, and I am staring at him, evoking the memory of endless hours on the floor, looking at my feet, the wall, my feet again, only now I am thrilled that the device I imagined is working, the silence is stirring up the audience and I, who knew nothing about drama except what I liked, have helped create a distinct and memorable theatrical moment.

The applause is powerful, and my joy is suddenly shattered, I want to weep and weep. I cannot bring my hands together, I cannot clap, I am unable to express and discharge my excitement the way I have always done, I am excluded from the audience. I will just sit here quietly during the interval, I could not take all the emotion, being looked at, greeting so many people, do I smile or look sad with each one?

I have a good friend at my side, it stabilizes me to know that I have a culturally knowledgeable companion who entered my world from nowhere as I entered hers, I am staying at her flat, we sit up till all hours talking about movies and love, then go to our separate bedrooms to have our separate dreams. She was one of the main organizers of an anti-apartheid cultural fund-raiser at which part of the *Jail Diary* was read and where, preparatory to making my first post-bomb appearance on a stage, I shared a dressing-room with the Leader of the Opposition and his wife, and nearly tripped over the foot of the playwright Harold Pinter as I moved through the wings – one way, I thought, of introducing myself to the forbidding English cultural milieu.

Someone has placed arms around my neck, I am being hugged with intense and loving pressure. I look up, and see a woman's face next to mine, short black hair, strong white teeth in a big smile against dark skin, South African accent, cultivated.

'Albie, it's me.'

She is holding me and stroking my shoulders and looking happily straight into my eyes. I do not recognize her.

'It's me . . . Dorothy.'

I struggle to stand.

'Dorothy!' I shout joyously 'Dorothy!' I will tell the audience about Dorothy, and the problem of how to end the evening is solved, if Dorothy agrees. I whisper to her, and she says all right.

The second act proceeds fluently, the audience is warm and encouraging, and responds especially strongly to the tricks and games invented to help the time pass . . . word-chains, from JAIL to FREE in seven moves

. . . JAIL . . . FAIL . . . FALL . . . FELL . . . FEEL . . . FEET . . . FRET . . . FREE. The alphabet of songs, starting with A . . . Always . . . I'll be living here always, Year after year, Always, In this little cell, That I know so well . . . B . . . Because . . . C . . . Charmaine, the songs of my adolescence, some of them now making a comeback on the wave of nostalgia. The Station Commander who was something of an expert on everything, including the exact age of the earth (5794 years), gets strong laughter, though he is played sympathetically, which pleases me.

The last scene comes through effectively, the actor playing Albie is running to the beach, six miles, he has never run so far before, he is elated, he has survived and now he is free, his friends are shouting his name as he plunges fully clothed into the sea. Moments pass, and he is being interrogated once more, it is two years later, and he has suffered torture by sleep deprivation, and this time he collapses . . . I wish the play could have ended on a less sad note, and yet this was the reality; when I left South Africa I was pretty crushed, I had not only lost some of my innocence, as I said during the play, I had lost most of my optimism.

The applause rolls on and on, the actors take bow after bow, and I am banging my hand on my thigh as vigorously as I can. The clapping swells to a highpoint that is held for a long time; this has been an unusual evening in the theatre, we all want to feel it has been memorable and special, and that through the actors and the producer and the playwright we are expressing our repudiation of those responsible for planting the bomb and our human solidarity with each other. The ovation continues and then suddenly stops as David Edgar walks on to the stage.

We have come to the last part of the evening, and I am still not quite sure what I will say. I know it will come out well, since I am filled with deep and loving emotion, my family is out there, and my surgeon, and the man from the BBC and physiotherapists and the administrator from the London hospital that did not wish to be named, and Wolfie and my lawyer friend Henry and my pal Sal and Lola and Merle and Joel and Gabs with whom I stayed after coming out of hospital, and Becky and Kenny who helped organize the evening, and everybody there has come specially to be with me, and if I cannot rise to the occasion I deserve to be sent to meetings for the rest of my life, and if I cannot make a good little improvised speech after having dreamed of it for weeks then I know I am dead.

Peter McEnery, the first Albie, if you do not count me, follows David on the stage. How easily he moves, speaking with his Royal Shakespeare voice in casual mode, reaching every single spectator without the slightest need for projection, turning gracefully to make the most of the stage in the round. I will be seated and will use a microphone, I dare not risk a repetition of Oxford. When I first met Peter I had the uneasy feeling that he could play me one day and Hitler the next, and I could not escape a semi-conscious resentment at this theatrical promiscuity. Yet now he is speaking with an intelligence and sensibility that indicate that I was not simply a limited season role for him, but a personage whose experience had intrinsic meaning. I do not usually wish to be like someone else, but I wish I had his posture, his easy way of talking without forcing, his capacity to revolve and glide around the stage as though just moving naturally.

It is now my turn. I heave myself up, and move

slowly down the steps. There is no hurry, people should have time to adjust to my presenting myself, I need a few moments to get the sense of the hall, of where the audience is and how I can reach everyone with my eyes. The applause gets more and more vigorous as I approach the empty chair on the edge of the stage.

Everybody is waiting, this is the moment where the evening ceases to be about a certain part of my life and actually becomes another part of my life, this is the highpoint of my year of soft vengeance. I lean forward towards the microphone, aware that it is the first syllable that counts the most, that vocal instant when you break the silence and establish yourself in the consciousness of those present.

'In the play the actor representing me says that in prison he lost some of his innocence.' I can hear my voice being amplified cleanly, I am speaking with soft and comfortable control. 'Now in some strange way the bomb seems to have blown that innocence back. In fact I seem to be dealing quite easily with the big things, it is some of the small things that cause me the most difficulty. One of them cropped up this evening. I cannot clap my hands. I wished to applaud all those responsible for this very beautiful performance, but could not do so in the way I wished, hearing the sound of my palms, feeling my flesh against my flesh. Yet I can overcome this problem, but I need your help in producing a good, strong sound. I am going to make some noise, to feel that I am clapping, but I would like this to be a tribute from all of us, so please help me.'

I am taking a chance, I have never tried this before, it is an emotional *salto mortal*. I lift my left hand, place it near my face, and begin beating my cheek. Clap, clap, clap, clap . . . the sound is not very strong, but it is flesh against flesh. The audience is shocked for a moment, and then the applause begins, strong, tense, staccato, and I turn my face towards the actors as I continue to slap my hand against it. Clap, clap, clap, clap . . . The applause is strong, too strong, I feel that I am forcing it a bit, but I know there are gentler moments to come. Some in the audience are gathering their programmes, the clapping becomes climactic. I put up my hand for it to stop and lean towards the microphone again.

'You all heard the whistling of the "Going Home" theme in the play. The whistler saved me, gave me courage at a crucial moment, reached to me through the metal and concrete. Only afterwards did I discover who it was. David Edgar made the whistler part of a composite character. The other half of that character in real life was imprisoned many times and he was eventually tortured to death, it was very tragic. I am happy to say, though, that the whistler, who was in fact a woman, is here with us tonight . . . Dorothy Adams, would you please come and join me on the stage?'

There is movement in one of the rows, everyone is looking round and as the audience see the figure of Dorothy enter an aisle and walk down towards the stage a burst of stormy, emotional applause fills the auditorium. I rise to greet her, we are both radiant, it is a wonderful moment in our lives, to be re-united before so many witnesses, expressing through this gesture our determination to survive all and see our people free. When I was in prison I often wondered what Dorothy thought of this white man coming along and involving himself in what she would have regarded as a black persons' struggle. In the few glimpses I got of her, she always seemed so composed in contrast to the turmoil I felt inside myself; she later told me that she had felt exactly the same in regard to me, how could I be so calm? We are hugging each other, revolving slowly like Peter McEnery did, this is our first time on the stage, and we are not black and white, just two people together, who love each other and their country, proof of the easy destructibility of apartheid. The applause could go on the whole night. I put up my arm for silence and go to the microphone, gesturing to Dorothy not to leave.

'There is somebody else present tonight whom you heard about in the play, the person at the other end of the telephone, demanding to know what was happening to her son, the person trying to send me clean blankets . . . Mommy, will you please join us on the stage?'

My mother rises, Alan and Michael and Stephanie are beaming, everyone in the audience is either smiling or crying and the applause swells to another ovation. Dorothy and I are standing shoulder to shoulder, my left arm around her back, her right arm around mine. My mother embraces first Dorothy then me, moves to take up position at my right side, remembers that I do not have an arm there, and graciously moves to Dorothy's left, where they clasp each other. The three of us turn slowly, my mom and I holding Dorothy in the middle, receiving a sustained ovation. The English are supposed to be unemotional but many in the audience are weeping, this is a specially wonderful night for us all, a night of mutual emotional recognition and support, and for me, a night of soft and joyous vengeance.

33

My toes are hitting the gym floorboards, my body is bumping and shaking, my whole frame seems to be in spasm, but I am moving forward, I am running. From the physios' desk down to the exercise bicycles, about twenty clumsy paces, but I am running. I have increased my speed from a snail's pace to that of a tortoise, but I am running. The regular patients lying on couches down the sides of the gym, flexing their knees, receiving heat on their ankles, lifting weights on their insteps, have watched me without watching for weeks now, accompanying my progress from the day when I could hardly get on to the bicycle, to the moment when, like a newly born colt, slender and unstable, I managed to lift myself from the floor, till the time when I had the courage to launch myself into a little run. Now I have done three lengths and I am sure I can do four.

Boom . . . crash . . . boom . . . for what I have in mind, I must be able to run, otherwise the journey will be a failure. I have spoken to the Ambassador, and he has said I will be welcome. I am telling nobody, but I must get myself ready.

My left foot, stiff with what the doctors call foot-drop, crashes clumsily down, my right ankle is still tender and rigid, I have to will my body forward with each step, but I am running. Each jolt against the floor provokes a shudder that travels through my knee-joints to my hips and up to my neck. Just half a length more, and I will have reached my target, I must keep going, even if I have no momentum, no flow, just this jerky propulsion maintained purely by will.

I have done it, four lengths, and I am sure I can do more. First I must lie down and have my little cry. Whenever I do something new, something physical in which my body gets shaken up, I feel a great need to cry, to let little shudders of grief mixed with joy pass through my body. I lay myself down carefully on a couch, my chest heaving from the exertion, cradle my head in my arm so that only my shoulders are exposed, and feel the quiet, tearless weeping begin. There is so much emotion trapped within me, so much distress at the damage to my body, inside and out, that I take advantage of these moments whenever possible, sometimes even in the most public of places, to allow the traumatized lava to bubble quietly away.

I am sure I can do eight lengths, I will have another try. I get myself into position, as if starting a race, count to three, and once more lurch forward. Crash . . . boom . . . crash. I must try to think of something pleasant, get my limbs and body to move automatically while my head is engaged with half-thoughts and daydreams.

A World Apart, what a beautiful movie, even though I could not speak for six hours afterwards, I was so stirred by the film about Ruth as viewed by her daughter. What a pleasure it is to see a work where everything is clean, the filming, the acting, the story itself, the evocation of her posthumous and our continuing world. I saw a review which criticized the fact that the focus was on a white family. There is truth in this. I sense that in this great Western world the loss of one white arm causes more shock than the loss of four black limbs, or even four thousand. All the more cause for those of us who have exposure to speak about the vast numbers of victims unknown outside their immediate communities, and convey to the world the damage caused to hundreds of thousands and even millions. Yet more important, conditions have to be transformed so that black artists can project directly their own experiences and vision of the struggle, as is happening in theatre and music and dance, with Miriam and Hugh and Abdullah, and as will soon occur in film, no not soon, it has already happened with *Mapantsula*, a vivid counterpart to *A World Apart*, made in Johannesburg by black and white film artists seizing their opportunities and working together. When I was locked up, it was a source of pain to me that privilege followed me even into solitary confinement. Now I acknowledge, but with less pain, the continuing reality that privilege pursues me even as a bomb victim.

Seven months have passed and everything about my life seems to be falling into place – well, nearly everything. Surviving the bomb was not a miracle, it was a question of angles and aerodynamics, and direction of blast forces, but solving my economic problems in London without money will be a miracle, and it looks as though, with the help of the Bishop and the International Defence and Aid Fund, the miracle will take place. A special fund has been created for me to receive a rehabilitation and re-integration loan on generous terms; the money is already pouring in, people want to give, it is coming from Canada and Sweden and Holland and Norway and many other parts, and my repayments will be used to establish a special fund for other less known victims of apartheid. So I was right to buy flowers.

I am still bouncing and flopping as I proceed down the gym, but feel that a certain rhythm is emerging and that I will be able to double the eight lengths to sixteen.

191

My breathing is heavy, but my lungs will last out, it is all a question of my thighs.

Even the question of my work is sorting itself out. Someone from London University asked me what I would like to do, and I said research relevant to the creation of a new constitution for a non-racial, democratic South Africa. Wonderful, she said, I am sure you will get funding from bodies like the Ford Foundation and the Norwegian and the Swedish Development Agencies . . . I am sorry I did not buy even more flowers, and feel more convinced than ever that those of us born into privilege should not waste time on despising ourselves but get on as robustly and effectively as possible with the job of pouring into the struggle everything we have been fortunate to acquire, our knowledge, our vision, our culture, while we enrich our lives with the one thing our privilege denied us, sensitivity to the culture and longings of the oppressed.

Sixteen lengths is nothing, I am going to double that to thirty-two, maybe to fifty. I am moving clumsily but well. I have the psychology if not the body of a jogger, and I recognize that I have reached that joyous moment when I cross the threshold of exertion and just move along, sensing I can go on forever.

One day, one day, white will be beautiful again. It was a Mozambican leader who said this: white is beautiful. His grandmother was African and his grandfather Portuguese, and when we asked him what his government felt about the phrase 'Black is Beautiful', he replied: 'Black is Beautiful, Brown is Beautiful, White is Beautiful.' That is what we want, in South Africa, everywhere in the world. White made itself ugly by declaring that black was ugly. Now ironically, it is black that will help white discover the beauty in itself.

This growing elation that I feel bodes well. I have been sluggish since my second operation. I noticed when I was preparing my first letter on a computer that the opening paragraphs written before the op. spoke about activity being like a moonwalk, whereas after the op. I had a great struggle to finish the letter. I have to get my head very clear in the next few days; what I am planning could be disastrous if I am not in the right frame of mind.

Boom . . . crash . . . boom . . . crash . . . My feet are clumsy, but I can feel already that fifty lengths will be easy, maybe I can double that. If I do a hundred, and each length is twenty yards, that means I will have done two thousand yards, a mile. I can do it, I know I can. Faith, will, an inner spark, whatever we call it, it is not just a question of discipline or being a good patient. I am the worst of patients, in that I did not do my exercises at home as I was counselled to do, but I am the best of patients because I lived actively, and the exercise came naturally. It was joy that enabled me to swim again, and it is intimations of joy that are helping me to run further than the physio will think proper.

My running shoes clomp heavily on the boards. Left foot, right foot, crash . . . boom . . . In a few days time I will be travelling . . . left foot, right foot . . . like a rich man . . . crash . . . boom . . . with lots of leg room . . . crash . . . boom . . . on a short visit . . . crash . . . back to Mozambique . . . boom.

FOUR

34

There is no sound as my feet plunge heavily but joyously into the sand, only the constant suck of the shimmering surf and my ecstatic gulping of air. My toes dig into the cakes of sand burnt dry by the warm sun after the tide retreated from this vast stretch of island beach. I am back, I am alive and I am free, and laughing wildly and triumphantly to myself on my relentless jog. I have left the boat and the bodyguard and my friends far behind, and feel I can labour my legs on forever. At some stage I must stop . . . perhaps when I reach that large bleached log that glistens in the sun . . . no I will just go a little further, to the point opposite the tree . . . well, just another hundred yards till I come to the outcrop of coral rock . . . I must stop, I can feel that I am slightly crazy, the sun, the sea, the return to Maputo, feeling sea-sand underfoot, I am completing my interrupted journey to the beach, and this is my victory run, alone with myself and the vast blue sky and the huge turquoise sea, and my footprints trailing on the deserted beach.

Apart from that, Albie . . . ha, ha, ha . . . apart from that Mrs Lincoln, did you enjoy the play? . . . apart from that, Mrs Kennedy, did you enjoy your ride through Dallas? . . . apart from that, Albie, did you enjoy your day at the beach? Bitter American humour, yet in my case the answer is: yes, yes, yes, I did enjoy, yes, yes, yes, I am enjoying, my day, my month, my year at the beach.

When I sneaked away on my run after our session of snorkelling above the coral reef, no one seemed to notice; even the bodyguard lay down on his towel to dry off. I loved floating in the water supported by a lifebelt, watching the myriads of blue and yellow and orange and black fish flashing in the clear tropical water, moving myself round in small circles as I stroked with my left arm, feeling elated that I had found the courage to slip over the side of the boat and launch myself on the ocean top.

I know everything . . . ha, ha, ha, ha . . . it is not funny, but it seems hilarious . . . I know who tried to kill me. He is about thirty years old, talkative, heavily built, with a little moustache, a black Angolan recruited into the South African Army Special Forces unit, who says he came into Mozambique about two years ago with explosives and a mission to kill me. I found this out by accident at a Christmas party. I was eating some chicken when I heard people chatting next to me: 'So they caught the man who tried to kill comrade Albie . . .' 'What?' I exclaimed . . . and then I learnt that some ANC persons, working with Mozambican security, had got on to him, and he had spoken freely of how it had taken a long time to get the bomb into the car. His superior was a white South African lieutenant who had got away and whom he had admired very much, and he also referred to a third person, who he claims actually put the bomb in my car, but he cannot describe this person, so our people think no such person exists.

I went to some high-ups, and with lots of apologies and explanations, asked if, er, could I see my would-be assassin? I do not know what I had in mind, it was just an immense curiosity to see him and confront him with my presence and procure some kind of human response from him. I did not feel any anger at all, just a wish to let him see me and to personalize the relationship, take away the terrible feeling that to him I was just an object to be eliminated as scientifically and coldly as possible. Perhaps I also had a secret desire to disarm him (interesting that that was the word that came to mind), and to encourage him to talk about his group and how they had operated (traces of my days as an advocate; one of my colleagues even said once, to my pleasant surprise, that I was among the best cross-examiners at the Cape Bar). But it was Christmas time, the Minister had just gone on holiday, no one was there to authorize this unusual request, and I never got to see him, so to me he is just a description.

Who knows what will happen to him, maybe he will be swapped, maybe he will be kept for ages without any decision being taken. I gave my views, but only indirectly, it was during a radio interview, ha, ha, ha, ha, no one but I knew the significance of what I was saying, how personal it was to me, and I told the interviewer that if ever the person responsible for putting the bomb were caught, my most fervent wish was that he or she be tried by due process of law in the ordinary civil courts, and if the evidence was not strong enough for a conviction, he be acquitted. It gave me great secret happiness to say that. The risk of acquittal was fundamental, since the creation of a strong system of justice in Mozambique, one in which the people had confidence, which operated according to internationally accepted principles, would validate all our years of effort, but more than that, it would be a personal triumph over the bomber, it would show the total superiority of our values over theirs, it would be the ultimate in my soft, sweet vengeance.

My shadow proceeds in front of me, bouncing over the tide-marks and pieces of driftwood, head and shoulders crunched together because of the overhead position of the sun, my left arm swinging in contracted shadow form, and my right arm missing. I am used to living without my arm, but I get a little shaken each time I see this truncated image bumping along the white sand.

I turn round and laboriously and happily lope back along my footprints. There they are in the distance, the security guy in his tight bathing costume – I wonder where he keeps his pistol? – our friends from Zimbabwe, and Lucia, whose scanty purply-blue bathing costume, the one we chose in Rio on our last holiday together, glowed to me like her personality. My chest is heaving, I have to pound my feet into the sand to keep myself going, but I am feeling so elated that it is not difficult to maintain my jerky rhythm.

I know everything, ha, ha, ha, I am euphoric . . . I even know why I felt so high in the hospital immediately after the operation, and why still today, despite the loss of my arm and some blindness and marks on my face (one of our comrades said the Boers had Africanized me with tattoos like Tambo), and coloured scars (that my pal Sal told me matched my eyes), I am feeling so good. Someone suggested that my sensation of existential élan was like a prayer in a godless world, a simple statement of relief and incredulity at having survived, but I feel it was something much deeper than that.

Ever since I was seventeen and sat down on a seat marked 'Blacks Only', I have been preparing myself for the bomb, not necessarily the bomb as such, but some confrontation with apartheid power, and always, consciously or unconsciously, I have wondered if I would withstand the test – would I survive? would I be brave? would I hold fast to my beliefs? This is what happens to you when you join the movement, you put yourself on constant trial, embark on an intimate journey with

200

your fear, self-doubt and courage. Your imagination feeds on the heroism of others, you imbibe poetry and read prison memoirs and participate in the huge oral tradition of struggle in which the feats of the brave and the clear-sighted establish standards of conduct and personal morality that both inspire and terrify you at the same time. The tension grows within you over the years. You are waiting for the moment of fateful confrontation, and wonder each minute of the day and night what will happen and how you will conduct yourself. My moment came, and I survived largely intact, and my instincts were strong and positive. It was helpful to be admired by others, but what gave me my sense of internal joy was the knowledge that I had myself that I was fulfilling my deepest longings and triumphing over my most intimate uncertainties. The culture of resistance has over the decades penetrated to my innermost spirit and given me the capacity to triumph. Even if nowadays all over the world the culture of popular struggle is undergoing a profound, necessary and at times confusing transformation, we can still look back with undeviating pride to earlier generations who moulded simple profiles of noble behaviour, and take deep satisfaction if our behaviour corresponds in any way to theirs.

They might try to kill me again, make it appear an accident, or plant someone in the organization to go for me, but I cannot be permanently on the run. That was why I came to Maputo, to conquer the possibility of secret dread, the sense that part of the world was forbidden to me, and the rest, the work I did and the people I met, is all bonus. So the bomb, being close to death, has not really changed me or my life all that much, if anything, I feel freer, lighter, looser. The first thing I did was pass by the spot of the explosion. I asked my colleague Gita to slow down the car and waited to see if my heart would go boom . . . boom . . . boom. Not a flicker, not the slightest tremor. The weeks since then have been full of . . . sadness . . . I spent a morning of deep emotion with the Mussagy family whose husband and father had died after lying in a coma for seven months . . .

. . . surprise . . . I did not tell anyone I was coming, just presented myself. It was easier for me that way, more spontaneous, people nearly fainted, said they thought I was a ghost, there were some tears, but mostly yells of happiness, at the hospital, at the homes of my friends, at work, but the biggest surprise was the one I received myself. It was after I had given an interview to Mozambican TV, and we were just about to go home when they told me it had been they who had pulled me to safety and it was they (one of them a close friend) against whom I had been fighting as they rushed me to hospital, so I turned the camera around and interviewed them . . .

. . . diplomacy . . . I received rapturous welcomes from Swedish and Norwegian aid representatives who would not believe that I was actually there, spoke to the Cuban Ambassador and colleagues who pulled out huge cigars and crowded round me to hear the whole story, drank tea with the American Ambassador on her residence balcony, the Stars and Stripes flapping almost in our faces (she told me she had prayed for me and once again I was moved), and dined and conversed happily with the British Ambassador and his family and then with the Representative of the Liberation Committee of the Organization of African Unity . . .

. . . blessings . . . every single one of the working

people I met, the clerks and cleaners and gardeners and chauffeurs whether they looked sad or radiant, said either: praise be to God! or Allah be praised!

. . . honour . . . the President, whom I have always liked as a person, called me in, spoke warmly with me for an hour, and said I could visit Mozambique whenever I wanted and be sure of a good welcome.

And I have my own welcome to issue. Welcome comrade Nelson to the brilliant white sand of Clifton beach, beautiful place of my childhood and of my dreams, across the sea from Robben Island, where you spent so many years, we can run there together at the water's edge, past the rocks, and heal the ocean with our feet. It is exactly a mile there and back, and Wolfie says you used to jog, even in the underground, we will have won the freedom of the sand under our toes, you, and all the others, and I too, unashamed in this post–modern world to call ourselves freedom fighters, and we can fill the beach with ex–prisoners and detainees and exiles and underground workers, for our generation is indestructible, and nothing can stop us. We are in motion, I am running, the people back home are going forward, my recovery and theirs accompany each other, we have all taken heavy knocks, I through the bomb, they through the State of Emergency, but we are all moving.

Life is good, the sun is hot, the sand tickles and scrapes against the soles of my feet, I run, therefore I am. May everyone in the whole world be a little mad and very happy forever, may the day come when all humanity walks around in bathing costumes without a place to put their guns, may the sun continue to warm the earth and the waves forever roll up against the shore.

New York, February–May 1989

Epilogue

Was it worth it?

A long, slow, totally intimate yet highly publicised run was the affirmative way I had chosen to mark my stepping aside from organized political activity. The mayor of Cape Town gave me a kiss and a gentle push with her hands to send me on my eleven-kilometer way, the traffic police cleared the road, television crews developed their calf muscles while they ran backwards to capture frontal images of my elated panting, a waiter handed me a small cup of espresso (not a banned substance) when my legs pounded step by slow thudding step into the pavement outside Giovanni's, and the workers at the Arthur's Seat Hotel shouted "Viva, comrade Albie, viva" as I jogged slowly and heavily past the palm trees on Sea Point promenade. The occasion was a repeat of my run thirty years before from Caledon Square Police Station to the sea. It was 1994, six years after the bomb, four years after my return from exile, and a month before the country's first free and democratic elections, and I needed to do something personal and physical to feel the involvement of my body in the process of transforming South Africa. The intense underfoot churning of the fine white sand of Clifton Beach was as joyous as I had long envisaged. As I eventually threw myself with narcissistic bravura into the cold waves, Basil "Manenberg" Coetzee, one of the creators of Cape jazz, blew his saxophone loudly—he and I and the gathering crowd celebrated the simultaneous recovery of my body and the revival of our country.

How necessary and yet how sad that my generation of freedom fighters had been compelled to transmute the painful and distinctive ecstasy of our lives into the run-of-the-mill emotions of any other contenders for office. The great and poignant paradox of our lives was that we had fought with all our passion to create a boring society. Although the quest for human rights would never end, the forms it took would now be different. I felt that we had won the right to embark upon new careers that had been unthinkable as long as apartheid was in place, and, much as I admired my colleagues from the struggle who were willing to carry on with political work, I wished to shout my last "Viva!" and be considered for appointment as a judge or, failing selection, to make movies. At the conference in a hot crowded hall to ballot for persons to be placed on the ANC election list, exhausted by nonstop travelling during the negotiation period, I had gripped the table in front of me and drunk several glasses of water to make sure I stayed awake. My fear had been that I would fall asleep before the Ss were reached and wake up effectively a member of Parliament. I wouldn't enjoy electioneering—vote for us, we've got the finest policies, we're the best, we're the most honest—as if integrity were something capable of calibration. I hadn't wanted to find myself anxiously waiting for a telephone call to see if I had been chosen for some high government post. At last I heard the words "Sachs, Albert Louis," stood up, and said "Please take my name off the list," and with this short sentence weaned myself from forty-two years of total personal commitment and disciplined loyalty to the cause. The values would be the same, but the context and format quite different.

As I eventually stood in line to vote I wished I hadn't felt so tired and tense, my sleep destabilized by the weight of history, my waking moments upset by a terror that some madness would overcome me in the voting booth and force my hand perversely and shamefully to put my cross next to (my vote was my secret) instead of next to (my vote was my secret). The elections were meant to be the most joyous period in my life, yet the only moment when I wept with real tears of unforced emotion was when I saw on TV the elderly and the infirm being the first to vote. [Mommy, you must live, we need your vote, there are special assistants for the blind. . . . My mother knew what I was saying: it wasn't the extra vote, it was a reminder of what her life of ninety years had been about, ever since as a rebellious schoolgirl she had sung: God save our gracious King, when we get hold of him . . .] Elderly African men and women stood with a quiet, disciplined sense of achievement and told the interviewers exactly what I knew they would say: we have waited our whole lives for this moment, and we, the crazies, the idealists, the holders of impossible dreams, turned out to be right, our lives were valid after all, our beliefs justified. Suddenly, for three days we had become the normal ones, and the rest of the disbelieving world the oddballs.

Yet the shock of having suddenly reached my life's most wondrous day seemed to have left me disturbed rather than elated. Shuffling forward in a queue to make two anonymous pencil marks, I was about to consummate the most precious asset any person can have, the hope for a glorious future, and at the same time to extinguish it. Could it be that once we achieved our ideals, we could no longer live for them? I felt miserably neutered by the normality for which we had fought, and which had produced not only the desired political equality between black and white but an unsettling equality of emotion and existence between ourselves and those who, offered a choice between human rights and a piece of chocolate, would have selected the chocolate each time.

I thought with amusement, part smug, part wry, about the one previous time I had received a ballot slip. It had been during my second detention, nearly thirty years before, in a doubly-padlocked cell in Roeland Street jail, and I was recovering from torture by sleep deprivation. To save himself the complicated routines required to unlock both padlocks, Captain Rossouw of the Security Police thrust his hand with the ballot slip in it through the bars of the window and said: Advocate Sachs, this is a democratic country and you have the right to vote, and I answered: No thank you, Captain Rossouw (we freedom fighters were well brought up), I would rather not, and I saw the ballot slip float back past the bars.

Now with my left hand which, disappointingly, would produce the identical feeble scrawl of my former right hand, I picked up the pencil provided in the voting booth, and thought of the words of Albert Luthuli, the ANC President who had died in banishment: After decades of knocking patiently and vainly at the door asking for improvement of our conditions, our life is worse than it was before, and the only road to freedom now lies via the cross. The cross on the ballot paper, the cross of sacrifice.

It hadn't just been the solitary confinement, the sleep deprivation torture or the bomb; it had been the surveillance, the bugs, the raids, the informers, the unrelenting pressure wherever we were, every hour of day and night, to wipe us out because we had the vision that one day in South Africa everyone would be equal. ("You mean, you seriously believe in one man one vote?") Truly, whatever else it signified, the Bill of Rights in our new Constitution was the negative biography of our generation, the "never again" of our lives. Our confrontations had been real and directly experienced: the suppressed panic, the unrelenting tension of underground work, the comradeship of the embattled, the pain of isolation, the constant secrecy that had compelled the most honest amongst us to become the biggest dissemblers. It had been dark and intimately and intensely our own, and, oh, so sharply and personally experienced.

[*Albie, I don't know why you want me to dictate my memoirs, I wasn't important. . . .* Mommy, that's exactly why . . . *I was able*

208

to get a visit to Albie while he was held in Caledon Square under the
ninety day law. Johnny had just undergone an open heart operation
in London and I phoned the police and cried over the phone that my
one son was in hospital and my other son was detained: so I was able
to visit him. I bought a new dress, and had my hair and nails done.
I came along looking as bright as I could. I never wore that dress again,
only that once. The visit had the opposite effect on Albie to what the
police had expected. They thought I would be crying and pleading with
him to talk, and what happened was the contrary. He wanted to say
something, and I put my hand to my lips because I was sure there
would be a microphone somewhere. After that we just spoke about
trivialities. Even though it was a chilly day, Albie chose to meet me
in the yard rather than in his cell, not only to get fresh air, but to
avoid being bugged, yet I was sure there would be a microphone there
as well. It didn't matter, though, it was enough just to see him. Later,
after his release, Albie wrote to Johnny about me, saying "poor
Mommy, her son the doctor went to hospital, her son the lawyer went
to jail."]

Today, I thought with dismay, my life and my smile were
becoming more public, while my emotions were growing ever
more private. Once upon a time our success had depended on
deep secrecy, now it flowed from intense publicity. Instead of
putting on gloves to hide fingerprints and be invisible from the
police, I would choose attire to make me look handsome, trust-
worthy, and wise on TV. What mattered was no longer the
intrinsic quality of the things we did, but the excellence of the
way we presented ourselves. Our emotions, once intensely and
rawly our own, were now parasitic on the experiences of others. Fevered by soundbites on the screen or radio or snippets
in print, we were unable, even unwilling to immunize ourselves against electoral cholera. We ended up investing the banal
exercise of counting ballot slips with the intense and over-
furnaced emotions of history. And just as our feelings came
from watching and reading about the doings of others, so did

the world at large witness with pleasurable disbelief the queues of black and white voters waiting patiently to participate as equals for the first time in our elections, and declare that our negotiated revolution was a miracle.

It wasn't a miracle. It didn't just come to pass. Our transition had been the most willed, thought-about, planned-for event of the late twentieth century. I had once written that all revolutions were impossible until they happened, then they became inevitable. In our case the movement from impossibility to inevitability seemed miraculous to many, particularly to those of little faith, who could only anticipate racial war and mutual ruin. That was the irony—the relationship between history and miracle had been reversed; for the total doubters, it had been a miracle, while for those of intense belief, it had been entirely rational. We believers knew that the transition had been the product of intensely thought-through planning and had been based on meetings and yet more meetings, endless, endless meetings, above-ground, underground, in prison, on Robben Island, in exile, meetings, some boring, some interesting, all with their "agendas" and "matters arising" and "any other business," meetings, meetings—I used to believe that freedom meant no more meetings, but still they continued, more and more meetings . . . we would have a classless society long before we achieved a meetingless one.

Did things just happen, or did we make things come about? I knew that nothing we were living through had just come to pass. We had willed it all, worked for it, never given up, never let go of the basic ideas. Yes, we had believed—belief had been fundamental—but we had backed it up with endless hard work, and learned how to do things together, and to accommodate the fears and interests of others, and to survive the sarcasm and disbelief of those who regarded themselves as more knowledgeable than ourselves about what they called the real world, and we just kept going on and on until at last the impossible became first feasible then real and finally inevitable.

I marked my clumsy cross next to the photograph of (my vote is my secret) folded it with my teeth, and dropped it in the box. Sufficient unto the day was the banal goodness thereof.

I did not know if I was sweating so much because I was driving a car for the first time in years, or because of the midsummer heat, or because I was about to go for the first time on a gay rights march. Shortly after my return to Cape Town I had been contacted by a group of lesbian and gay activists from the anti-apartheid movement who asked me for my suggestions on the best strategy, as they put it, to combine social emancipation with sexual emancipation. My suggestion had been to follow this sequence: first decriminalize, and get rid of the laws which punished gays for doing what straights were allowed to do, then equalize, and bring an end to discrimination in employment, housing, and so on, and finally create the conditions to live freely and differently in all spheres of life. In other words, don't start with gay domestic unions, but end with them. Giving advice had been easy, but being asked to join the first gay march in Cape Town, well . . . . I wanted to propose a special section under a banner Straights for Gays, and immediately felt ashamed. I was uncomfortable driving my new red Honda—automatic gears, a swivel on the wheel, indicators on the left—through the heavy Saturday morning traffic. The roads of Cape Town had changed in the three decades since I had last driven there, there were new overpasses and one-way streets and places where you could no longer turn, and the traffic was much heavier. The organizers had said we would assemble at the usual meeting place, and I had been too embarrassed to say that this particular great freedom fighter didn't even know where that was. So I was late, and I knew they would be disappointed, thinking I had ducked out, as no doubt they thought I would do in the ongoing constitutional negotiations—who would worry about gay rights when there were so many great issues of overcoming apartheid to be dealt with?

Fortunately, I did have some knowledge of the area. One of the first things I had done after coming back was revisit sites of marches and meetings from "the old days," like the Grand Parade in front of the City Hall, where we used to meet Saturday afternoons with a microphone mounted on a truck, my serious speeches being interpreted into Xhosa and the audiences roaring with laughter as the interpreter gave his own input. (Archie, what was so funny, all I said was that we needed world peace? Comrade Albie, the people don't want peace, they think if there's another war they can rise up against the whites, so I told them that if we had another war, the Russians would send a bomb to blow up Dr. Malan in his Prime Minister's residence, but then it would blow us all up as well.) We had stopped at Caledon Square Police Station: so pleasant to be able to walk in and out at will, with a sense of triumphant moral authority, even if it meant passing the soundproofed room in which during my second spell of detention I had been kept awake until I had collapsed on the floor and had water thrown on me and my eyes prised open by heavy security police fingers. Finally, we had gone up to the barren spaces of District Six, the area that had been destroyed so that a whole community could be forcibly removed because they were not white, and I had communicated to the journalists who accompanied me my feelings of shock at being in the void where I had formerly visited friends in a throbbing neighborhood, but not told them that mingling in with the anger was a quite different and unexpected feeling, one of infinite amazement that the tar and the buildings had been removed, that the land was able to breathe again, that the slopes were once more joined to the looming mountain from which they had been detached, and that a new and harmonious city for the repossessed, organically related to the land, would grow there again.

During all the years of exile in London, like Heine's frozen fir tree dreaming of being a tropical palm, I had longed to be driving in the Cape Town heat with my back sticky against the seat, but now the sweat was extremely discomforting, and again like the poet's baking palm, I wished I was back in the snowy north. At last I heard some distant drumming, then I saw the banners and the throng coming towards me. There is something about people claiming their rights that always stirs me, the more so if they open up the streets and replace the anonymous metal clutter of traffic with the warm corporeality of surging human bodies. Men holding hands, women with their arms around each others' shoulders, individual cross-dressers proclaiming themselves in bright clothes, posters, banners, slogans being shouted. . . . Oh, no, I'm not going to march next to that one, "Suck, don't swallow," with my picture in the paper tomorrow, oh, no! I had been looking forward to being in an open-air demonstration again, after the years of nonstop negotiation meetings in airless rooms, arguing, debating, fighting, agreeing, consulting, referring back, getting a mandate, finding a solution, words, words, words, which represented our lives, and those of generations past and generations to come. Yet I was late, the march had already started, and my car was pointing in the wrong direction. To go through so much agony and not even join the marchers would have been the ultimate defeat. Compulsively spinning the knob on the steering wheel, sweating heavily, I tracked their whereabouts by their receding noise. The problem was to find parking, and the only open space was the yard reserved for personnel of the St George's Cathedral—forgive me, fathers and mothers, I cannot say I knew not what I was doing—I rushed through the Public Gardens to the long, processional avenue outside Parliament, caught up with the back of the column, moved forwards rapidly past "Suck don't swallow," and found myself happily next to law professor Edwin Cameron, now a superior court judge, and suddenly felt myself to be as gloriously free and proud as I had felt at any time since my return to the country. I had broken the invisible barriers of alienation that had kept me physically apart from the gay community even while declaring my full intellectual solidarity. I felt especially happy that I had made such an important breakthrough in my life while walking up an ancient and beautiful avenue lined with oak trees.

"Dear friends," the people listening to me in front of the microphone at the edge of a bandstand were clearly curious, "ending the march in this park has a special meaning for me. As a child I used to play here, a beautiful place with grass and trees and a glorious view of Table Mountain. The whites-only signs came later, and they've gone now, but what a disgrace it was to tell people that because you are who you are, you cannot walk your dog here, or wheel your pram or throw your tennis ball or sit on a bench and read a book. Yet there were other signs, not as visible, but enforced with the same ferocity. If you happened to be attracted to or loved someone of the same sex, you were also told to keep out, this beautiful place was not for you, unless you pretended to be someone you were not." Not only were the couples listening intently, but even some of the cross-dressers who had deliberately marched at a different rhythm from the rest, and who had seemed irritated by what they regarded as the formalism and pomposity of speechmaking appeared to be attentive. "But the question of human rights for homosexual men and women is not just one of eliminating injustices against a section of the community, of acknowledging fundamental human rights. It is also about the nature of the country we are all going to live in. Until now, people have always been told how to behave, what their rights and duties were. Everything was prescribed. Behaviour was forced, hypocrisy was rampant, and oppression abounded. What we want is a country where we can all live in equality as we are, with our languages, histories, tastes, beliefs, and orientations. We are entitled to enjoy the right to be different, as far as our lifestyles and personal choices are concerned, and to exercise the right to be the same, with respect to our dignity and citizenship." The cheers were long, the speeches were short, and I ran down the hill to retrieve my car, hoping that it had not been towed away, or, worse still, that it did not have under the windshield wiper a note in stern prelate's language informing me that I had conducted myself with extreme disrespect for the Church.

I had hardly slept the night before, not because I was going to be talking to the people who had tried to wipe us out—I had rather welcomed meeting them in the open and as equals—but because of my fear that through naivete or overeagerness I might be responsible for betraying the hopes of the millions of South Africans who could not bear to be disenfranchised and oppressed any longer but who were also exhausted by endless years of struggle and pain. And I could still remember the recent, sad prediction of a woman activist friend of mine: all that will happen is that power will be transferred from one gang of men to another.

The first day was particularly draining. All the men on the ANC side wore suits, the women were soberly dressed, and the one delegate with a baby at breast (now a cabinet minister) restricted her feeding to the moments when she sat in committee. The men from the government ranks also all came in suits, mostly very dark; there were hardly any women in their group, but there were a number of smokers, who soon got together with the smokers on the ANC side, as had the non-smokers and anti-smokers on both sides, the first nonparty alliance! Yet the heaviness and uncertainty lasted only until the actual work began, drafting a Declaration of Intent to establish an agreed conceptual basis for the negotiations. I spoke up: I was so eager for our Constitution to be the first in the world to proclaim itself non-sexist, that as soon as the all-party drafting committee accepted the phrase "South Africa shall be a non-racial state," I suggested that the words "and non-sexist" be added. There were no women in our small group, and the white men, including the chairperson, were all bemused by the phrase and claimed not to understand it. I responded that if they did not actually object, they should let it in, since it had real and powerful meaning to people from the side I was representing, and was neutral as far as this group was concerned. I seemed to be isolated and felt an awkward strain in the proceedings. No doubt they were thinking that some people were born politically correct, some achieved political correctness, and some had it thrust upon them, and that in my case must have been all three. Perhaps they were right, at least from the age of six I had found myself standing firm against the tide, anchored by a sense of immoveable moral certainty. The only time I could remember screaming with spontaneous rage at my children was when I had come across them taunting a neighborhood kid. "Fatty, fatty, run away fatty—" "Don't you ever dare—" I had yelled at them, beside myself, and so unaccustomed had they been to hearing my voice raised that they looked at me in amazement. In England I had written a book on sexism and the law in which I had tried to analyze why it was that for sixty years British judges had denied women the right to vote, to study medicine, to practise as barristers, and to take up seats on a town council, and had done so through the legal device of holding that women were not "persons." I had found myself developing a special affinity for the suffragettes whose strongest weapons had not been guns or money but their willingness to go on hunger strikes and confront the state simply with their will and their bodies. Now I could still remember the recent, sad prediction of a woman activist friend

216

of mine—all that will happen in the negotiations is that power will be transferred from one gang of men to another.

It was embarrassing and lonely to be so insistent, but I decided I would accept being outvoted rather than voluntarily back down. Then one of the black men said that the womenfolk had fought hard for change in South Africa, and that life was difficult for our mothers; he felt the words should be included. The other black men supported him. There was an uncomfortable stalemate. Two black men and me (what was I?) against three white men. Oh well, said the chairperson with some irritation, just to save time we could put the words in and leave it to the plenary session to decide what to do. Some hours later we had a rough draft of the document ready, the very first negotiated text of the formal constitutional proceedings. Triumphantly the chairperson and I polished the grammar and general layout. "It's ready, we've done it," said the chairperson, aglow, as I was, with a sense of historical moment. "We need to have it typed—" He looked around. "Let's give it to one of our girls." I mumbled bravely that the person to whom we gave the manuscript was a most accomplished underground operative who had evaded capture by a huge army of police, and not a "girl." The next day we produced another text and the chairperson looked around again: "I think it's ready for one of the—" he hesitated, knowing he had to be careful, "—one of the lassies." I gave up

As it turned out, the phrase "non-racial and non-sexist" survived the plenary. To my initial joy, it appeared in the first draft of the interim Constitution; to my consequent dismay it was later replaced by a formulation that incorporated much of its substance but lacked its symbolic resonance, and to my eventual delight it was reinstated in the final Constitution. The last shall be the first. Together with outlawing discrimination based on disability or sexual orientation, including environmental and socio-economic rights, and emphasizing that South Africa was to be guided by the values of an "open" society—a word I had insisted on—the Constitution declared that the democratic state of South Africa was founded on the values of non-racialism and non-sexism. And I had been one of the founding parents!

Nelson Mandela raised his tall frame, and took out his glasses. The dignitaries had squeezed into their allocated places, the cameras were in position (no arc lights, please, the President's eyes were damaged during the years he worked in the limestone quarry), and, as the person in charge of organizing the ceremony, I was pleased that all was proceeding perfectly. "The last time I stood up in Court," he told the tightly crammed audience, "was to find out if I was going to be hanged." His voice was slightly hoarse, and he looked around for a moment. I could see what he wanted but couldn't move. . . . The President cleared his throat and continued, "Today I rise to inaugurate South Africa's first Constitutional Court . . . ." Damn, amongst all the arrangements I had forgotten to provide for a glass of water.

My main personal preoccupation related to a small but worrying matter of conscience: how should I take the oath? Should I affirm or swear to God? Two of my colleagues affirmed, the others lifted their right hands and swore the words "So help me God" in Tswana, Xhosa, Zulu, Afrikaans, and English. If I affirmed, I would not raise my arm, while if I swore the oath in the name of the Deity, I would. I had grown up in a home where conscience and belief were everything, and where the transcendent was to be found not in an imagined creation or hereafter, but in the directly experienced earthly real; to take the Lord's name unbelievingly for anything at all was to take it in vain. At different times in my life I had had intense experiences of otherworldliness, even occasional out-of-body sensations, and friends had often said that I was religious by nature if not by formal belief. Yet the world itself was so spiritualized and full of awe and wonder, and the need for goodness so self-evident, that there seemed to be neither space nor necessity for the existence of a separate metaphysical realm invocable through submission or prayer. At the same time, I had been the one who had insisted, during the three relentlessly gruelling years of negotiations, on including the words Nkosi Sikelel' iAfrica—God watch over Africa—in the text of the new Constitution. The opening words of the anthem of sacrifice and hope had united the nation, believer and nonbeliever alike, and for the great majority of South Africans had invested the Constitution with an indispensable sense of solemnity and rever ence. Yet one's conscience was that most precious part of self that related to one's innermost personhood, and had little to do with what was lovely or convenient or consoling to the world at large. The President of the Court looked at me. It was my turn. "I, Albert Louis Sachs, swear that as a judge," I lost my concentration and stumbled . . . "of the Constitutional Court I will be faithful to the Republic of South Africa, will uphold and protect the Constitution and the human rights entrenched in it, and will administer justice to all persons alike without fear, favor, or prejudice, in accordance with the Constitution and the law." I knew intuitively the way to make my most truthful commitment, to the Constitution, to the values it enshrined, to the memory of my friends, Looksmart, Loza, Babla, Ruth, Jeanette, Joe, Dulcie and all those who had been martyred so that we could live in a democratic state based on respect for human rights. I pushed upward the heavy, dark green sleeve of my new gown, with its red and black cuffs. Under the eyes of the President of the country, the Deputy President, the Speaker of the National Assembly, the Chairperson of the

Senate, the Chairperson of the Constitutional Assembly, judges from all over the country, my family, and the millions watching on television, I raised my stump: "So help me God."

My son Alan, who had refused to wear a suit and tie but was elegant in a stylish shirt, came up to me afterwards in the milling, touching, hugging, kissing crowd. "Dad, you hesitated. . . ." The new, emerging, ebullient elite, colorfully dressed, physically expressive, mingled with the more reticent and somber old guard, who smiled courteously all the time but never laughed out loud. Judges who had been comfortable when passing death sentences and upholding emergency regulations were now engaging in friendly small talk with colleagues who had irritated the old regime by their independent refusal to follow suit. Mandela enjoyed some banter with the person who had supervised his last years in prison. Wives and husbands and children were introduced to each other—"This is Stephanie Kemp, my former wife, and my children Alan and Michael . . . and my brother Johnny. . . ." [*I am very disappointed, Albie, you should have given me the choice, even if you thought I couldn't manage the flight to Johannesburg. Anyway, the decision has been made. There will be lots of us at Highlands House who will have our TV sets on, and the others can tell me what's on the screen. I get congratulations every day, and I ask what have I done, you are the one who deserves the congratulations, I am only your mother.*] There was much surprise that I could have children, a brother, a former wife. Someone had actually once come up to me and said he was amazed to see me walking in the street. "Congratulations," I heard from all sides. The formal photographs were taken, we still had twenty minutes of mingling before we would walk over for lunch, everything was going according to plan, those years "in the struggle" of organizing activities down to the minutest detail bore good fruit that day. "Congratulations, you deserved it. After what you've been through, you deserved it." Again and again I heard these words:

"Congratulations, you deserved it." How well meant, and how hurtful all the same. It just was not like that.

As my well-wishers saw it, I was being elevated to the bench as a just reward for all the years of endeavour (for backing the right side?) and as appropriate compensation for the injury I had received. Yet had they asked me straight out, Do you think it was worth it, after suffering the loss you did, on this your happiest day, ending up as a member of the highest court in the land? I would have answered no. The idea of measuring my involvement in the antiapartheid struggle in terms of personal reward was deeply distressing apart from the implication that one could be appointed to the court not on the basis of capacity but for time served. What had given honor and dignity to our lives was precisely the fact that we chose to combat injustice without thought or even hope of receiving personal benefit. The reward was in the endeavor, the comradeship, the fervor of human interaction, the sense of living an intensely meaningful life that engaged fully with the world while establishing a distinctive personal space for each one of us. In that sense we were the most privileged of all human beings in the late twentieth century, privileged to have taken part in a struggle animated by the highest ideals of the age. To regard the office at the end of the journey as its validation was to rob it of all its inherent virtue. Yet if the same questioner had asked: Was it worth it, after all you had been through, to end up tired and strained in an anonymous voting queue and be one of twenty million people making a cross on a piece of paper, I would have answered yes, yes, yes. The reward was the journey itself, the ineffably rich human encounters on the way, the manner in which we evolved, so interesting, so full of surprise, so challenging emotionally and intellectually, as we led three, four, five, six lives in one. We dared everything, had views on art, science, the origin of the universe, the nature of history, the destiny of humanity. Everything tied up. Once you invested your life in belief, everything that touched on that belief became meaningful. Our love, our anger, our romanticism, our fantasies, all had a special intensity. We were not somnambulists meandering vacuously through life, but human beings incandescent with purpose. Many of the ideas that gave us strength turned out to be based on lies and cruelty; at times our individual personalities got confused and bruised in the collective; we suppressed real sides of ourselves in the name of an abstract greater good; we were often incapable of expressing personal love or enjoying beauty for their own sakes; we could act with the arrogant self-confidence of the self-nominated agents of history; we had as many personal disasters and heartbreaks as anyone else, at times even more. Yet there was always that distinctive experience of participating body and spirit in something meaningful, the sense of engaging with the deep passions of society, of being linked to something intensely virtuous, of overcoming the barriers that kept human beings apart, of responding to and joining in the deep music of African humanity. Finally, at the end of it all, or, rather, at the close of the particular stage that had overwhelmingly occupied our lives, we were accomplishing our goal of living in a free, nonracial, and democratic country. This was what made sense of our lives and justified everything. This was the meaningful reward to which we felt entitled. This, and not attaining office, was our soft vengeance.

"*Verskoon my*" [Forgive me]. A heavily built man was blocking my way as I moved towards friends in the club Rosie's and All that Jazz. I moved aside, and once more he stood in front of me "*Verskoon my,*" he said again. Raising his voice to penetrate the sounds of the band warming up, he explained that he was part owner of the club, and wished my forgiveness for . . . he looked at my arm. I struggled to answer him in Afrikaans, but years of exile had left my linguistic memory incomplete, and

Portuguese words mixed themselves into Afrikaans and English in my reply. *Hierdie bonita club is jou verskoning* [This lovely club is your forgiveness], I answered. I then pushed my way through the throng to sit with my friends, while he went to the managers' table, and we glanced discreetly at each other, both discomfited by the encounter. What I wanted to say to him was: Don't ask me for forgiveness, I knew what I was doing, I made my choices, if you want to ask forgiveness, don't request it from the one white person whose trauma you know about, ask it of the millions of persons of color who had no choice, whose oppression was enduring, all-encompassing, much deeper than mine, and who are still forced to exist in unliveable conditions. Furthermore, the mere fact that you are Afrikaans-speaking doesn't in the slightest make you responsible for what the government did, even if it had claimed to be acting in your name. If everyone was responsible in general, then no one would be responsible in particular. Yet even as these strong and confused thoughts passed through my head, I regretted that I had not simply put my arm around him and given him a big hug of acknowledgment and acceptance.

This forgiveness thing was so complicated. Why was it that those who had the least to be ashamed of were the ones who did the most to seek forgiveness, while those responsible for the most egregious conduct tended to be the most recalcitrant? Why could they not simply acknowledge that apartheid was not just a failed social experiment but an evil, cruel system that had bitten into people's souls and destroyed their bodies? Especially when, as Archbishop Tutu, head of the Truth and Reconciliation Commission set up by the new democratic Parliament in its first year, was to point out again and again, such acknowledgement would have been met with a hugely generous response.

Ironically, the idea of setting up a Truth Commission had emerged from a fierce internal debate inside the ANC some months before the elections, on what to do about ANC camp guards in Angola who had ill-treated captives under their control. It had been a harsh but rewarding debate; I recalled Samora Machel's statement that to know the taste of an avocado pear, you had to cut it in half. An inquiry set up by the ANC had recommended that action be taken against these guards. Some, myself included, argued strongly that this be done—if you were fighting for justice, then justice had to exist in your own ranks. Others pointed out that the guards were young and untrained, working in circumstances of war against a ruthless enemy. Then someone asked what his mother would have thought about the situation. She would have said that the ANC was mad, punishing its own people when the villains who had murdered and tortured for decades in defense of apartheid were getting off scot-free. That was the moment when Prof. Kader Asmal (now a Cabinet Minister) proposed that after the elections the new government should commit itself to a Truth Commission that would look at all violations of human rights from whatever quarter.

As the constitutional negotiations advanced, the quality of our accommodation improved, starting from an uncomfortable and vulnerable motel in Lusaka and ending up at the Holiday Inn at Johannesburg Airport. The negotiations completed, I found myself back in the spartan lodgings provided by the Catholic Institute for International Relations in London, not unhappy to be out of contact, for the first time in years, with the negotiators, not even a fax machine in the place. Then someone shoved the text of a fax under my door. The elections were in jeopardy; leaders of the security forces had declared that they knew of plots to bomb the elections out of existence, and that they were willing loyally to protect the electoral process but not if they were going to go to jail afterwards. They insisted that they had been promised an amnesty as part of the program of enlisting their support for the negotiations process and safeguarding the transition to democracy, and now they felt they were being betrayed, would I contact Cape Town urgently to give my views on what should be done. I wasn't even able to get paper to write on, so I set out my views on the back of the message and faxed them off the next day. Appropriately, my last act as one of the negotiators of the constitution was to work on the text of a post-amble, leaving the way open for an amnesty for politically based offences but only to the extent that full disclosure was made by each individual applicant. It was not necessary to spell out the precise details in the post-amble— once the principle of amnesty was constitutionally guaranteed, it should be left to the new democratic parliament to lay down the procedures and conditions that would govern the way it should be granted. It was this hastily produced provision that opened the way to legislation for a Truth and Reconciliation Commission, which in effect was to grant amnesty in exchange for truth.

Every few months I received a new story about who had put the bomb in my car, with just enough detail to destabilize me but not enough to clear up the matter. The fullest account came from an Afrikaans-speaking journalist who tracked down the person who, with professional pride, claimed to have masterminded the attack. This person was indignant about the whole affair, which, according to him, had manifested great injustice. He explained that the operative whom he had sent in had done an outstanding job—it was true that he had not killed me, but he had managed to make soup out of my arm. But the head of special forces, a terrible bloke to work under with no sense of fairness at all, had paid this brave operative a pittance, while he had given four times as much to a favorite of his who had not even attacked his target, but merely placed a death notice in the newspaper and collected his bounty. Where, he wanted to know, was the justice in that? My next piece of information came from a right-wing Member of Parliament next to whom I was sitting on a flight from Johannesburg to Cape Town. He told me he knew who the would-be assassin was, a real bad egg, now running a garage shop not far from Cape Town, who had told him that what saved my life was the assumption that my Honda had been the normal right-hand drive, whereas in fact it had been a left-hand one. (This was true, my car had been one of a small batch imported directly from Japan). Then, one night at Manenberg Jazz Café, I was introduced by the manager to a good-looking, well-dressed young man, very drunk and preoccupied with himself, who told me he was the son of a world-renowned French clothes designer, had been a mercenary working with South African special forces, and knew well the person who had tried to kill me, in fact he had killed that person himself. Hearing him above the noise was not easy, his head sagged and his speech was slurred. He seemed to want some angry reaction from me, and to be irritated by my mentioning that the phase of fighting was over, that we had all to get on with our lives, and that it no longer mattered very much who the actual individual was who placed the bomb, what was important was that we all worked together to make our country better.

The next account was different. I was put in touch with a woman who seemed lively and self-possessed on the telephone, and who told me she knew who had tried to kill me. We agreed to meet. She had an attractive presence, looked as though she could have been a systems analyst or buyer of specialized merchandise, and clearly was fascinated by me, just as I was by meeting her. She indicated that she was completely surprised by how gentle my manner was, not at all what she had expected, and went on to tell me that an ex-lover of hers with whom she had been deeply involved had boasted of having had a hand in the attack on me. Our encounter was strangely intense. She and I seemed to be locked into a narrative that invited exploration of hidden areas suffused with sexuality and death. It was clear that she had challenged life and lived unconventionally, and that, like myself, she was feeling shocked by the sudden intimacy of our encounter, two total strangers united by an absent third person, the man whom she had physically loved and emotionally hated and who had blasted my body without even knowing me. She and I spoke once more on the telephone, but never met again.

The one concrete piece of information I was to get came a long time later. It was from a former special services operative who visited me in my chambers, saying that he was intending to apply to the Truth and Reconciliation Commission for amnesty with respect to his part in the attack on me. He insisted that his role had been limited to preparing photographs of my car, that commandos had landed from a ship in Maputo bay, that he had dropped out of the project some time before the attack because of the lack of professionalism by those in command, that the intended target had been my friend Indres Naidoo and not myself, and that I had been saved because the liquid explosive they used had not been tilted at the right angle. All the time he spoke he seemed to be comparing himself with me, as if to say that the only difference was that he had been on the side that had lost in the end, while I had ended up on the side that had won. His original military jauntiness with me disappeared. He had been wounded, like I had, he told me, but had been forced out of the military by the old politicians, was without a regular job, and had lost the gratuity paid to him when he had invested it in an arms importation venture with Eugene de Kock, who had recently been sentenced to hundreds of years in jail for murder and fraud. I felt curious about him, and was pleased that he had come to my chambers to look me in the eye, even if his motive might have been to get a statement that could assist his application for amnesty. I told him that the time to speak to me again would be after he had testified to the Commission, that he could make a contribution to the whole country by telling the full truth, and that I could not speak about forgiveness or offer him a handshake until that was over. He seemed ineffably sad, although he managed a jaunty stride once more as he walked away.

I received yet further information from what seemed to be a convincingly anxious voice on the telephone, giving names and details about special force operatives who claimed to have been responsible for the bomb attack. . . . The stories were so varied and came from such disparate sources that I was left confused. They were not all incompatible with each other, since diverse people could have been involved at various stages. Yet the actual identity of the persons concerned seemed to matter less and less to me. Did it make any difference if he (I assumed it was a man) was tall or short, young or old, black or white? or spoke English or Afrikaans or Portuguese? It would not have made much sense for someone to come to me and say: I'm sorry I blew your arm off. How could I respond? What I would have liked would have been to hear someone stating exactly what he had done, expressing regret that people like himself had found themselves dedicating their energies to war, hoping that it would never happen again, and indicating his willingness to contribute towards the building up of the country for the benefit of all who lived in it. I decided that if the matter was raised before the TRC then naturally I would show an interest, but that I would not myself engage the TRC with my story, which had already been told a hundred times. In the meanwhile, I passed on all the information I received to the appropriate authorities.

On my overseas trips, I was shocked by the sharpness of questions raised about giving amnesty to persons guilty of gross violations of human rights. I sometimes felt it was a case of: Vengeance is mine, saith the Human Rights Community. These were my friends from exile days. We had denounced apartheid together. Now they were condemning us. Perhaps it was because I had so little regard for imprisonment or the payment of monetary compensation as meaningful mechanisms for ensuring moral accountability, that I found myself reacting impatiently to the critique. With firm moral certainty but not without discomfort, I explained that there had been no question of the perpetrators simply granting themselves impunity. On the contrary, the victims had been party to the arrangements; the objective had been not to cover up the crimes of the past but to install democracy and constitutionalism, so that violations could never occur again; the evidence for successful prosecutions would be hard to find; the courts could be clogged up for years with trials and appeals which would probably end up with a few of the small fry being punished while the major figures got off without a scratch; and the TRC was serving a number of profound socio-moral purposes, all of which I regarded as being more valuable than sending a few villains to prison. It had three separate structures. The first simply gave the victims a chance to tell their stories. As Archbishop Tutu, chairperson of the TRC, explained, it was there for the little people whose terrible indignities had never been publicly acknowledged. A separate section would deal with reparations, which could include some financial support, but would consist most importantly of intimately personalized actions such as a proper burial and headstone for persons who had disappeared, or scholarships for the children of persons who had been assassinated or tortured to death. The third section granted amnesty to the perpetrators, provided their actions had been part of political conflict and they told the truth. The human rights activists listened patiently; they were not convinced, and pointed to the fact that many of the families of those killed were opposed to amnesty. How strange it was: the actual survivors of imprisonment, torture, and brutality were willing to forgo punishment of the perpetrators, while the families of those who died were not.

A lawyer friend had once said enthusiastically to me that I

should sue the bastards who had blown me up. I asked him how much he thought my arm was worth: a thousand, a hundred thousand, a million, a trillion? I was distressed at the idea of even attempting to put a market value on pain suffered in the quest for freedom. It was easy, of course, for me to refuse to sue for damages, or, later, to refrain from applying for a struggle pension or seeking reparations through the TRC. I was well-employed for the first time since I had left the university, my life was sufficiently structured for me to know what I would be doing the next week without having to read the newspapers. I had an income which was sufficient for me to live on comfortably and also to help my sons with their education. As a judge I was even entitled to hire a car from the state to get me from my Johannesburg lodgings to and from the court each day—instead of asking for a Mercedes or a BMW, which judges had always done until the president of our new court had opted for a Toyota, I had requested a Honda. Yet if my life had been less secure, it would have been morally even more important that I never benefit in any material way from the pursuit of my ideals. As a young advocate I had refused to take fees in the civil rights cases which had been the core of my practice (and, incidentally, I had been severely criticized for this by veteran ANC leader Govan Mbeki, who had told me that once all political activity had been banned, raising funds to pay the lawyers was the only way that the community could be reached). Each of us from relatively privileged backgrounds, who had felt a need to overcome not disadvantage but advantage, had our particular personal conceits that could not always be justified objectively but that had been subjectively meaningful to ourselves. My particular vanity had been to believe that the integrity of my involvement in the struggle had come from its being based on moral choice, always and only, and never on material gain. In the years when the only rewards had been jail, torture, death, or exile, this belief had not been put under strain. Now that the freedom fighters were out of jail, back from exile, and in office, new dilemmas would inevitably emerge. Each one of us would face them in our own way; putting my own position crudely, I wished in a rather old-fashioned way to retain my amateur status as a freedom fighter.

Judges don't cry; Archbishop Desmond Tutu, chairperson of the TRC, does. As a lawyer, I was puzzled and delighted at how much truth was coming out under his leadership as compared to the narrow and fragmented findings that criminal proceedings presided over by stern judges could have produced. I became suddenly alarmed at the comparable inadequacy of criminal trials. Then I consoled myself that trials had a much more limited purpose, and were about punishment and proof, not about reconciliation and truth. No one should be sent to jail without scrupulous attention to due process of law. This meant preparing precise indictments against individuals and subjecting all testimony to rigorous cross-examination and evaluation so as to avoid error. In the case of the TRC, on the other hand, the truth-seeking was of a much more sweeping character and the guarantees of veracity would be different. If we wanted our common citizenship to be worth anything we had to overcome the practice of having a white history and a black history, resulting in two completely separate and unreconciled accounts of what had happened in our country; we needed all to be on the same existential map for the first time, to cease once and for all being settlers and natives with different and incompatible destinies. This required not simply decontextualized, static, accurately focused microscopic truths, but broadly located, mobile, multilayered and interactive dialogic truth. When the victims testified, they did so not to get a conviction or to receive compensation or as a part of a campaign of political denunciation, but simply as a means of breaking the silence in which they had been trapped for so long. The atmosphere was humane and supportive in a way that courts rarely are. Proceedings might start with a prayer or a song; there were comforters to put an arm around the shoulders of weeping narrators; the Archbishop himself cried. The stories poured out with a detail and emotion that could not have been manufactured. The other stream of truth flowed along a different course. It consisted of the narrations of the perpetrators, who were testifying in their own words to what they had done. They were not witnesses in show trials who had been tortured by the security police into making confessions: they were the security police. They came not from detention cells but as free people in their suits, with their stiff security-force body language, their lawyers in attendance, their carefully prepared statements, and sometimes, their apologies. In many cases it was they, and not just their victims, who were receiving treatment for post-traumatic stress disorders. Their motive was to get amnesty. They had no reason to admit to things they had not done. Grim validation of the veracity of their stories had come from the discovery of bodies of persons they had secretly buried. Documents had come to light. Internal corroboration on an extensive scale had been provided. The truth, or at least some of the truth, about the killings of prominent activists such as Steve Biko and the Cradock Four, emerged for the first time, after ordinary legal proceedings had turned up next to nothing and left relatives of the murdered persons even more distressed than they had been before. Reconciliation would take a long, long time, and for our generation would never be total, but at least the foundations were being laid. The findings of the TRC would outlive those of the ordinary courts of law, but the due process of law would outlive the TRC.

The jets of water were icy on our backs. A bath person, then a shower person, then a bath person, I was now a shower person again; it was easier under the jet to shampoo with only one hand, and my backaches seemed to have disappeared completely since I had followed advice to end my ablutions with cold streams of water following the hot. She screamed and laughed, while I just tautened my mouth. We seemed to be different in everything—in age, in background, in temperament, in experience, even in the way we reacted to cold water. Of all the women I had loved, she had two things that were different: she smiled when she woke up in the morning, and her hands were rough from having washed and scrubbed since she had been a child. She claimed that she had fallen in love with the narrator in *The Soft Vengeance,* and I couldn't help feeling proud of that person and a bit jealous of him at the same time—how could I ever match up in life to the character in the book? What made me aware of my love for her was seeing her brush my mother's hair and file and polish her nails and give her the spontaneous physical affection that I felt too inhibited to offer. [Mommy, she's about your height, with a round face, Indonesian features, people regard her as pretty, even beautiful, and she always sparkles, and is as kind to her dad in hospital as she is to you; like you did, she left school to help the family, saved up to go backpacking and then skiing in Europe, she's saved some money from her work and has her own house in Hout Bay where not all the people welcomed her arriving in the area, and when I asked her what she'd really like to do, she said there were eight brothers and sisters sleeping in one room, and once a year they would pack picnic baskets and walk to the station and take the train to the only beach where people of her color could go, and as the train went through the white suburbs with their beautiful houses and gardens full of flowers and trees, she said to herself when I grow up I am going to build houses like these for everybody, and now she has gone back to finish high school and has invited me to her end-of-year ball, and I've accepted, and next year she'll be studying architecture at the University of Cape Town.] Years before I had been sure that I could only marry someone who had been in solitary confinement; now I felt the opposite, that I wanted to be in a world without the accumulated pain of struggle, to share with another my days and nights not only physically and legally as a free, unburdened, and unbruised citizen, but emotionally too. My crowd had never had problems loving our neighbors. Now slowly we were learning to love ourselves.

The marquee was incongruous in the middle of the Old Fort prison, yet it provided a suitably secure and festive enclosure within which President Mandela would announce the winner. Who, people wondered, had come out first in the international competition to design a new Constitutional Court building? The proceedings were started by a slender person, slightly shorter than the microphone in front of her. Why did she look so familiar? I had met people on so many continents at such different moments of my life, or, rather, of my many consecutive lives . . . who was she? She waved a special greeting to me, then lowered the microphone, and still I could not place her. "My name is Lulu Gwagwa." Lulu! Of course, it was just that the context had been so different, one of our last meetings in exile, organised by the Women's Section of the ANC to discuss and take positions on all the hard questions: the family, abortion, homosexuality, sexist practices and abuse of women in our own ranks, affirmative action, broad gender sensitivity rather than special women's rights. "As Deputy Director in the Ministry of Public Works, it is my duty to introduce a large number of speakers to you, and also to see to it that they don't go on and on in the way that senior government personalities and judges are wont to do." Lulu had given the best expression of African feminism I had ever heard—how could I have forgotten her? She had introduced the debate on the family, and argued that our enemy was not the institution of the family as such but refusal to recognise the different ways that families were constituted and the unequal relationships within the family. It was encouraging to see people like her in senior positions in the administration, not just because of her manifest intelligence and knowledge of the world, but because she came from a generation that had been fired up by black consciousness, imbibed non-racialism and non-sexism, learned how to work patiently with anybody and everybody, and realized the importance of functioning in a structured and coherent way with a long-term vision.

The speakers obediently gave short and well-focused addresses, the celebratory mood being maintained by Lulu's relaxed introductions. She was buoyant with the President too. "Mr. President, it is your turn now. Since you are the main speaker, I will allow you an extra few minutes. . . ." "Thank you, Lulu, I appreciate your indulgence and promise not to abuse it." Then suddenly the pleasantries stopped, and Nelson Mandela's expression became stern. "I have given strict instructions to my security guards," he began, looking seriously at us, "to get me out of here as soon as possible." There was always a strange pleasure in hearing his distinctive voice, even if it was rather grave at that moment—so many comics had imitated it, and with such fidelity, that whenever he himself spoke he seemed to be simply confirming the accuracy of their representations, not quite as good as some but better than most. In his person, with his humor, humanity, and clarity of thought, he was the great destroyer of the myths of racial superiority, the more so because of his serenity and ease. It was amusing for us to see that the whole world came to be photographed next to Nelson Mandela: the Queen of England, the Pope of Rome, Helmut Kohl, Bill Clinton, Jacques Chirac, even Michael Jackson and the Spice Girls; we too enjoyed having our pictures taken with him. "I feel quite uncomfortable at this moment. To begin with, I am in dangerous company, surrounded by jailbirds. I see Judge Albie Sachs sitting over there, I don't feel safe with people like him around." A few uncertain eruptions of laughter. "Then to add to my already distinct sense of unease I realize that we are in the middle of a notorious prison where I and thousands of others have spent various parts of our lives. I am always afraid that someone will lose the key and I will find myself back inside again." He was smiling now, and we all laughed loudly, not with the sycophantic mirth that so often greeted attempts at humor by those in power (there is no bigger lie than to laugh at a joke that is not funny), but with the spontaneous amusement we felt; it was a joy to be in the company of a leader who could pass off decades of imprisonment in such a generous and non-angry way. Just as Nelson Mandela had often made it clear in public that he was proud to be president of a country that had a Constitutional Court unafraid to strike down his own acts if necessary, so with the warmth of our response were we indicating our pleasure at functioning within a framework of constitutional values that he had done so much to promote. He became more serious. "One of the blessings we all enjoy is that we now live in a country governed by a Constitution that is admired throughout the world. The rights and duties of every person in the land are protected by that Constitution, whether he or she is the humblest or the highest. As you know, I was recently subpoenaed to appear in the Pretoria High Court to give evidence about my reasons for appointing a Commission of Enquiry into the affairs of the South African Rugby Football Union. My legal advisers told me that an important principle was at stake, that a president could not fulfill his constitutional duties properly if he or she was constantly being called to give evidence in court. No doubt they were correct, but I believed another very important principle was at stake, and that was that no one is above the law. As president I thought it important to set an example. I hope my legal team, who are truly brilliant people, will forgive me."

I thought then of the many long journeys we all had had to

make to reach the point where the Constitution would be central to our lives. As a child I had never had any special desire to be a lawyer. I had wanted to discover microbes smaller than anybody had yet seen, or fly to the moon, or find the source of an unknown river. [*Albie was about seven when he came home from school one day, having completed his first "legal" case. One boy had been accused of stealing. Albie wasn't convinced that the boy was guilty. So he asked him some questions and proved that he was innocent. The boy gave him some chewing gum, his first legal fee.*] Later, out of a vague sense of social responsibility, I had decided to become a lawyer so that I could defend people in distress and help secure justice. During my student years at the Law Faculty at the University of Cape Town, I found myself increasingly sceptical about the professors' theories on constitutionalism, fundamental rights, and the rule of law. I could not see how the world of legal rationality signified anything to the poor and the oppressed who lacked full political rights or access to economic justice. Not far from the University were the shacks of tens of thousands of working people for whom the law meant police raids on their homes in the middle of the night and constant harassment and humiliation in the streets during the day. At the same time, the people in these shacks had an energy, vitality, humor, and sense of hope which I never encountered on the campus. I would be asked to sneak into their areas at night to conduct study classes. The candles lighting up their cheekbones and eyes gave an intensely human and mobile aspect to the discussions. I discovered a sense of shared humanity and energetic quest for justice in every way more pungent and immediately meaningful than the elegant but seemingly arid formulations of distantly erudite English legal scholars. We spoke about our vision of a non-racial South Africa with a longing and sense of passionate certainty almost totally absent from the abstract logical discourses in my law classes—what logic gave, I thought, logic could take away, yet the hard and

237

dense emotion of lived endeavor was forever. As I saw it, on the one side were words about justice and exams to be passed, and on the other a real struggle for justice in a world of passion, engagement, face-to-face humanity, wit, song, prayer, and direct and courageous confrontation with a cruel state. Every year I would hitchhike up to Johannesburg and be reinforced in my convictions by the sparkle and engaging energy of the "Indian Youth" at Kholvad House, who informed me with amused seriousness that after the Revolution there would still be a place for lawyers, but not a very important one, and be confirmed in my views by the warmth of the few minutes I would spend drinking tea with one of the partners in the country's first black legal partnership, Mandela and Tambo. ["I wish we had more time to hear about the struggle in Cape Town, comrade Albie, but as you can see, the whole of the townships and half the rural population seem to be in our waiting rooms, and we have to do what little we can to attend to their needs, even though we realise that it is only through political action that most of their problems can be solved."]

Nelson Mandela paused. "I now come to the moment that has brought us all together, the opening of the envelope containing the name of the winner of the competition. Jeff, just help me here . . . Thank you. And the winner is . . ." He stopped, paused, reached for a glass of water—we all laughed— "and the winner is . . ." he had obviously watched the Oscars, "and the winner is . . . OMM Design Workshop from Durban in association with Urban Solutions of Johannesburg!"

It was my experiences in revolutionary Mozambique that showed me how important the rule of law actually was to the poor and the powerless. There had been much theorizing about the importance of people's power, which, my rights-sceptic legal colleagues had said, gave far more real protection to the poor than did so-called human rights, the mere playthings of lawyers. Yet I could see that in practice people's power could often be incompatible with people's rights, and that what was needed was a system that guaranteed achievable rights to all. The better-off persons had their connections, could bribe or threaten the police, and did not need the law. It was the poor persons whose husbands or sons or aunties were locked up who needed to be protected by secure rules and procedures. So it was that when we came to design the new Constitution for South Africa, the phrases of my law professors which I had once found to be hollow came flooding back triumphantly to me. The campus world of rationality suddenly merged with the shantytown universe of passion, and, far from the two fighting, each seemed to require and enrich the other. I had come to have no doubt that the idea of protected rights could be enormously empowering in a country where there was massive and systematic disadvantage based on race and gender. It was also necessary to accommodate difference in an open and pluralistic society, to ensure that homosexuals, disabled people, and all those targeted for discrimination because they did not conform to a stereotype of normality, could live in dignity. We had to guarantee workers' rights—how proud my Dad, Solly, would have been, recalling his struggles as leader of the Garment Workers Union from the twenties to the fifties—the rights of the child, language rights, cultural and religious rights. . . . In any event, there had been so many examples of exemplary freedom fighters ending up as heads of authoritarian regimes that institutional checks and balances against over-concentrated power had to be built in from the beginning.

A few minutes later Lulu waved to me again. "Albie, it's your turn now, the program says that you are about to thank the President on behalf of the Court for opening an envelope." I corrected her. "You've got it wrong, Lulu, I will give thanks on behalf of the competition jury, and my colleague Pius Langa will offer thanks on behalf of the Court." The idea of holding an international competition had come from an architect friend,

Jack Barnett, who had once, while himself in detention under Emergency Regulations, completed one of the many designs for buildings awarded to him through competitions. Jack had said that South African architecture had lost its spirit completely, and that only a competition could unlock the creativity of younger architects. It would also help avoid his greatest fear, that the cronyism of the old government would be replaced by a favoritism of the new. Jack had died not long after our conversation, and I wished I could pay tribute to him as one of those intellectuals who never lost faith in the freedom struggle, and pick up on the fact that Mandela had stayed at his house on that extraordinary day when Mandela had been released. But we had to be brief.

I explained that a year's hard work had gone into designing the brief for the competition. The jury had consisted of distinguished architects from India, Sri Lanka, and England, plus three South African architects, the mayor of Johannesburg (who had been locked up in the Fort), the Chairperson of the Commission for Gender Equality (who had also spent time there), and myself. (To our delight, the Englishman said it was the best jury he had ever been on, since the lay members argued so forcefully and insisted on the concept that was the most adventurous rather than the one that was the safest.)

I had listened to the President so many times, and now, still smiling from the interchange between Lulu and myself, he was looking up at me and waiting on my words. There was something concerning his relationship with the Fort precinct that I wanted to slip into the speech. So I had to try to get the tone just right in the new South African style, gracious, friendly, direct, humorous, serious but not solemn (or was it solemn but not serious?). This was not the moment to make my usual wry comment about the Fort—that we South Africans were proud of the fact that we possessed the only prison in the world where both Gandhi and Mandela had been locked up. I mentioned

240

that the winning design had been chosen because of its sensitivity to its special setting, its strongly South African feel, and the interesting friendly, and accessible character it promised to have. It would be the flagship building for the whole precinct, which would become known as Constitution Hill and provide amenities for scholars and human rights activists from every part of the country, as well as an attractive environment for people living in the crowded neighbourhood. It was hoped that a community of artists from Soweto and the northern suburbs and all of the country would be involved in ensuring that the ambience was suitably entrancing. Plans were afoot for bodies such as the Human Rights Commission, the Public Protector, and the Commission for Gender Equality to take up accommodation on the Hill. The biggest human rights library in the country would be there, as would the papers of the constitutional negotiations, "and the suggestion has been made," I glanced down into the President's eyes and slipped the words in, "for the Nelson Mandela papers to be housed there as well." He looked back at me in a surprised but noncommittal way; clearly he had not yet heard of the idea. "We judges come and go," I continued. "All of us here are mortal," I realized that this was not too tactful a statement, "except for the President, who will live to be two hundred years old. . . . The building will survive us. It will symbolize the continuity of the new constitutional order, just as the surrounding prisons will serve as museums to remind us never again to allow people to be treated as they were in the past."

As I walked back to my table, flushed with the applause and the exuberance and symbolism of the occasion, I felt that all the themes of my life had come together, this time in uncomplicated fashion. We were living in a constitutional democracy, I had a position on what I had no doubt was the most interesting court in the world, and in the midst of all this, I had been given a chance to play a part in helping to promote the

241

evolution of a new South African architecture, whatever that was, that would correspond to the new South African democracy. If I had been asked at that moment: was it worth it? without doubt I would have overcome my puritanism and answered yes.

It is good to have pride in honorable achievements. Yet there is more to it than that. I used to wonder sometimes if it were notionally possible that some countries could have more history than others, and if so, whether South Africa would head the list: over the last hundred and fifty years we had had colonial conflict, industrial class warfare, battles between language communities, even religious strife. The term "imperialism" was coined to extol British colonial policy in our area. The Anglo-Boer War gave rise to the phrase "concentration camps." We had also contributed to the world the word "apartheid"; indeed, no other country could claim that a whole international convention had been drawn up just to eliminate a policy which it had uniquely developed. Hopefully, we will one day see the word "ubuntu" also taken up by the international community, the term in our new Constitution that represents respect for the intrinsic dignity that each individual possesses simply by virtue of living with other persons in a community; trying to explain the concept to non–South Africans, I always suggest that if one could harmonize faith, hope, and charity with liberty, equality, and fraternity, and give it to an African choir or a mixed African-Afrikaner choir to hum, then you would have ubuntu.

Some countries are so established that the only way individuals can feel they have a real identity is by dimming their consciousness of the reality around them and lighting it up with a world of pleasure or imagination in which they can play meaningful parts. Yet other lands are so imploded and internally destroyed that there are no meaningful personal choices available

242

to them at all. In South Africa, on the other hand, there is an historic openness and suppleness of institutional texture that makes life intensely interesting, and fills it with extraordinary choices. Part of the pleasure of living in this country today is its openness, the feeling that it can go any way, and that each one of us can still have an influence. Nothing is ordained, yet nothing is out of reach. For many, this freedom is disconcerting. They would rather live complaining under the firm authority of a powerful state, which, love it or hate it, would take all decisions for them, than slowly achieve security through the growth of a richly textured, multi-universed, and organically vibrant society. They fear the openness of freedom and resist taking responsibility for their lives. At the same time, even those of us most proud of the freedom we have won are saddened by the absence of physical safety. I joke that it takes me exactly fifteen minutes to get to work each day: ten minutes to switch on and off all the anti-crime electronic devices to enable me to leave my home, and five minutes to drive to the Court. We have won our personal liberty but not our personal security.

It seems, then, that although we are good at doing the impossible, we are not so smart at accomplishing the ordinary: We are still far away from creating the boring society of our dreams, of turning South Africa into a safe, dull haven like . . . (my examples are my secret). Yet we have a strong and admired constitution, we are establishing the institutions of democracy, our economy is being restructured with a view to takeoff, we have a resilient trade union movement and influential religious bodies and professional associations which cut across cleavages of ethnicity, background, and color, which means that there are innumerable counterweights to the state, and, equally important, multiple counterweights to the counterweights. The inequities in our society are still immense. We might need another "miracle" to achieve decent living conditions and a sense

243

of equally open horizons for everybody. If so, we will accomplish it in the same rationally directed way as we achieved the last one: lots of belief, as much accommodation and flexibility as possible, endless boring tasks, courage in the face of resistance and ridicule, and adherence to certain simple and manifestly just principles. Only in this manner can we bring together all the little fireflies of miracle that flash and fade in the heart of each one of us, and produce something glowing, enchanted, and worthy for us all. More than anything, we have to find a way to curtail the incidence of violent crime that robs us of the right to walk and drive freely in our country.

For me, the twentieth century ended when my mother died in her ninety-second year. She had been born at the time of the 1905 Revolution in Russia, had come as a baby to Pretoria, and had embraced much of the passion and drama of the globe through her involvement, from adolescence to old age, in the struggle for human dignity and social justice in South Africa. [*When I was thirteen, my younger brother was killed by a lorry. This had a profound influence on me. The company wanted to pay my parents about two hundred pounds compensation money so that we wouldn't take them to court. They said it would alleviate our poor circumstances and help to educate the five children, of whom I was the eldest. I was furious and said my parents shouldn't take the money as it was "blood money" and it wouldn't bring him back. My father could have taken the money and not told me, but that would have been against his character. As far as I know, he never laid a charge either.*] Though eventually blind and unable to care for herself physically, her mind and humor remained spirited until the end. She had been elated when her elderly and frail neighbours in Highlands House had congratulated her on her son the lawyer being made a judge, just as she had been deeply proud of the achievements of her son the doctor who had become a distinguished medical scientist. She had loved the occasional visits from members of the ANC Women's League who had kept her

244

informed of their activities. The one thing she had insisted on during our last visits was that she not be buried or cremated, but that her body be donated to Medical School. After she died, I learned that getting into Medical School was not easy, not even when you were dead. The official concerned indicated that there would have to be an examination: the body could not be too obese, death must not have resulted from an infectious disease, and the body should not have been subject to trauma—could I return the next day? Twenty four hours later I went back with some anxiety to the mortuary to get the news: it was good, my mother had passed! Goodbye, Mommy, revolutionary typist, you never lost your desire to be helpful nor your spirit of personal self-determination, you led a long and honorable life, and you contributed much to the new South Africa. I feel proud to have been your son and to have lived much of my life according to your emancipatory values, the noblest of this brilliant and tortured century.

Cape Town, October 1998

Timeline of Major Events
in the Life of Albie Sachs

1935	Born in South Africa.
1957–66	Practised law in Cape Town.
1963–64	Detained in solitary confinement by security police, wrote *The Jail Diary of Albie Sachs*.
1966	Second detention.
1966	WENT TO LIVE IN EXILE IN LONDON, wrote *Stephanie on Trial*.
1967–70	Completed doctorate at Sussex University.
1970–77	Taught law at University of Southampton.
1977–83	Professor of law in Mozambique.
1983–88	Director of research in justice ministry in Mozambique.
1988	CAR-BOMBED IN MAPUTO, MOZAMBIQUE.
1989	Taught at Columbia University, wrote *The Soft Vengeance of a Freedom Fighter*.
1989	Founder-director of South Africa Constitution Studies Centre at the Institute of Commonwealth Studies, University of London.
1990	RETURNED FROM EXILE TO SOUTH AFRICA.
1991–93	Participant in negotiations for a new Constitution for South Africa.
1994	FIRST DEMOCRATIC ELECTIONS IN SOUTH AFRICA.
1995	Sworn in as a Justice of the newly-created Constitutional Court of South Africa.
1995–98	Truth and Reconciliation Commission functions.
1997	Mother dies aged 92.
1998	Helped design new Constitutional Court building.

Persons Mentioned in the Narrative

JACOB ZUMA, formerly ANC representative in Mozambique, now Deputy-President of South Africa.

JOHN NKADIMENG, former trade union leader, now ANC ambassador to Cuba.

MIRIAM MAKEBA, HUGH MASEKELA, ABDULLAH IBRAHIM: South African musicians who achieved international fame while living in exile.

GOVAN MBEKI: ANC leader imprisoned with Nelson Mandela. Father of Thabo Mbeki, who was Deputy President when the Epilogue was written and is now (1999) President of South Africa.

LOOKSMART NGUDLE, ELIJAH LOZA, BABLA SALOJEE: friends of mine who were tortured to death by South African security police.

RUTH FIRST, JEANETTE SCHOON, JOE GQABI, DULCIE SEPTEMBER: friends of mine who were assassinated by South African hit squads while living in exile.